Del Delker

Her story as told to
Ken Wade

Pacific Press® Publishing Association
Nampa, Idaho
Oshawa, Ontario, Canada
www.pacificpress.com

Edited by Deanna C. Davis
Designed by Dennis Ferree
Cover photo supplied by The Voice of Prophecy

Additional copies of this book are available by calling toll free
1-800-765-6955 or visiting http://www.adventistbookcenter.com

Library of Congress Cataloging-in-Publication Data

Delker, Del.
Del Delker : her story / as told to Ken Wade
p. cm.
ISBN: 0-8163-1951-0 – paper
ISBN: 0-8163-1965-0 – hardcover
1. Delker, Del. 2. Gospel muscians—United States—Biography.
I. Wade, Kenneth R., 1951- II. Title.

ML420.D45 A3 2002
782.25'092—dc21
[B]   2002035893

02 03 04 05 06 • 5 4 3 2 1

Contents

Chapter One

The Sunday anthem at the Evangelical United Brethren (EUB) Church in Oakland, California, was almost over, and my heart was skipping beats already. Soon the choir director, my good friend Bonnie Barnett, would sit down. So would the other nineteen members of the choir, and I would be left standing alone. Then I would have to make my way to the pulpit without tripping on any of the three steps leading down from the choir loft. I would have to place my sheet music on the pulpit without letting the congregation see how much my hands were shaking. And then I would have to open my mouth and sing *Ave Maria*, in Latin without losing my place or missing any notes.

There was a break in the choral portion of the music as the organ built toward the grand climax, and I took three deep breaths and reassured myself that I could do this. It would, after all, be good practice for what I really wanted to do with my life—sing with a dance band. Maybe if I could get through this song without fainting, it would help me overcome the stage fright that had up to now paralyzed me and kept me from trying to sing in public.

I had always loved music and often sang for my own amusement. But this would be my first solo performance before an audience—that is, if you didn't count that time back in Java, South Dakota, before I was old enough to have stage fright.

My mother, Martha Hartman, was born of solid South Dakota German stock out on the cold, windswept prairie of the northern United States. She grew up to be a beautiful young woman who attracted the attention of a lot of the young men. When she was twenty-three years old, one fellow in particular took an interest in her and decided she ought to be his wife.

Andrew Delker was a devoted Christian young man who sang tenor in the church choir and in a quartet. But he belonged to a different denomination than Mother, and she told him that she felt the difference in their religious convictions could cause problems in their marriage. He said he didn't think it was all that important and promised to look into what she believed. He probably thought he could change her after she married him, and she may have thought the same about him. Anyhow, he managed to persuade her to marry him.

Of course I wasn't there at the time, so I don't know much about just how the courtship went, but frankly, it reminds me of the fellow who once proposed to me. When I hesitated, telling him I needed more time to think about it, he suggested that I ought to marry him in haste and repent at my leisure. I found out later that I probably would have done plenty of repenting if I had let him persuade me. He was not known for being truthful.

With Andrew's smooth promise tucked away in the back of her mind, Mother marched down the aisle and became Martha Delker on March 20, 1919. Within a year, the union was blessed with the birth of a baby boy—Elmer Stanley Delker—who always went by the name Stanley. But by that time, Andrew's attitude toward Martha's religion had changed. He no longer wanted to accommodate her. It is my understanding that Mom went to her church alone most of the time. The religion thing caused a lot of conflict in the home, with his parents telling him, "A woman should follow a man's leading. She is not the head of the house." With that kind of pressure, it was natural for him to try to do everything he could to bring his wife under control, and apparently sometimes their confrontations became violent.

This change of attitude was a big disappointment to my mother, and a year or two after Stanley was born, she decided that the marriage had been a mistake and moved back home with her parents.

That was a big disappointment to Andrew, and he began trying to persuade her to come back. He'd do better, he promised. And she decided to give her marriage a second chance—after all, Jesus does teach us to forgive those who have sinned against us. He also said, "What God hath joined together, let not man put asunder."

But things didn't go a whole lot better the second time around. By the time Stanley was four years old, Mom's tummy was bulging again, and I was starting to kick around inside and give her morning sickness. When Mom was eight months pregnant with me, Andrew got into a fit of temper and beat her up pretty bad. I've been told that he was so violent that it was only by the grace of God that there wasn't a miscarriage or at least a premature birth as a result. Mom contacted her brothers and they stood guard while she packed her things. Then she took Stanley and moved out on her own, and I ended up being born into a single-parent home.

Life was not easy for a divorced woman with two children, but fortunately we had family nearby to help out. That wasn't enough, though, to keep us kids completely under control. And that's how I ended up with my first solo singing gig.

Mom told me that from the moment I began to walk, it was almost impossible to keep track of me. I had an uncanny ability to disappear, but usually I'd turn up an hour or so later—if I got hungry or something. Then one day when I was three years old, she went looking for me and couldn't find me. As the hours passed, she grew more and more desperate and soon had all the neighbors looking for me.

Then the phone rang. On the other end was the manager of the local bank. "Martha, are you missing something?" the banker asked.

By this time Mother was in tears, but she managed an answer. "Yes!" she said. "I can't find my daughter. We've looked all over for her. She's gone."

"Well, she's down here, standing in front of the bank, singing for a living, and people are putting money in her hot little fists!" he said.

Needless to say, Mother was there within minutes. She gathered me up in her arms and carried me home, putting an end to my singing career for the time being.

Since then I had sung mainly in the bathroom, living room, and kitchen, usually with an audience of one—myself. Music was a big part of my life, though. Mom said that my first babysitter was a record player. She could put music on, and I would sit and listen for hours. I seem to have had some strong opinions about music, too, because the family has often teased me about the time we were in church, not long after I had learned to talk, and the song leader got up and announced the opening hymn. But it wasn't the song I wanted to sing, so I just piped right up with *"Nein! Nein! 'Gott Ist die Liebe'!"* ("No! No! 'God Is Love'!"). We spoke German in our little church, and even at that early age I wanted to sing a song about the love of God. And the amazing thing is, I got my way. The song leader changed the opening hymn, and we sang my selection, with me belting it out at full volume. Before the song was over much of the congregation had broken out in laughter, listening to the little ham!

By the time I was ready to start school, Mom had decided that there just wasn't much future for her in South Dakota. She had been separated from her husband since before I was born, and the divorce had been finalized before I was two years old. But in those days there wasn't much enforcement of alimony payments, so Mom ended up trying to raise her two little ones all by herself. I do remember my father coming to my school one time when I was in kindergarten or first grade. He picked me up and said, "I'm your daddy," and gave me a quarter. That's the last quarter I ever got from him!

When I got home, I excitedly told my mother, "I have a daddy, too, just like other little girls!" I couldn't understand why that made her burst into tears! After that, he never ever contacted me until many years later when I received a letter addressed to me at work. Andrew Delker wrote, saying he had heard a woman named Delker singing on the radio, and he wondered if it could possibly be his daughter.

It was hard for me to deal with the feeling of being rejected all those years by my own father. It wasn't at all easy for me to answer that letter in a Christian spirit. But that's a story for later.

In discussions around the family table back at her folks' house in 1931, Mom and two of her sisters had come to the conclusion that things might be better if they would head for the Golden State—California. I don't remember much about the move, but it must have been like something out of *The Grapes of Wrath* or maybe *The Beverly Hillbillies*, although we didn't take Granny and her rocking chair along. Mom and her two sisters, Emma and Liz, plus Liz's husband, Bob Meckler, and Stanley and I all piled into an old car and headed west. Mom had only fifty-nine dollars in her purse, but she was determined to find a better life for us.

The money ran out in Yakima, Washington, and our traveling troupe had to stop. The trouble was there didn't seem to be any way to make money. The country was in the depths of the Great Depression. Jobs were about as easy to find as hens' teeth.

Bob went looking for work. Liz went looking for work. Emma went looking for work. They all came back with the same discouraging report. No work available. "Well, let me have a try at it," Mom said. Up to that point she had been staying with the car and our luggage because she had her two kids to look after.

Mom was nothing if she wasn't determined. A tenacious fighter, who often held two or three jobs at the same time to keep the family together, she never gave up on anything easily. By the end of the day she had found work for herself and the three other adults at a local fruit cannery. It was hard, backbreaking, dirty work, and it didn't pay much, but at least there was enough money for a few groceries. Fortunately a kindly man who had recently lost his wife agreed to take Mom, Stan, and me into his small house at a very low rent, so we had a roof over our heads. I'm not sure just how long we stayed there—probably just until the fruit harvest was over—but thanks to that man's kindness and the hard work of Mom and her siblings, we eventually had enough money to finish the trip to California, after a brief stay in Salem, Oregon.

That's how I ended up in Oakland, standing in front of the church, taking deep breaths, preparing to sing, at age twenty. The deep breaths seemed to restore my confidence a bit, and by the time I arrived at the pulpit, I was feeling a little more sure of myself.

Maybe too sure, judging by what happened next.

Chapter Two

Church wasn't my favorite haunt in those days. I guess I thought of myself as Thoroughly Modern Del. I spent more of my time in theaters, dance halls, and even taverns than I did in church. It wasn't that Mom hadn't tried to raise me right. She even sent me to church school for part of my educational career, but I had an independent streak in me right from the very start. The school I attended in eighth grade had pretty strict rules about dress and appearance. One thing that wasn't allowed was bright colors of fingernail polish.

Well, of course, that left me with the question, Just how bright is bright? Light pink was obviously OK, but it was hardly visible, so I tried a darker shade. No one seemed to object. Next time I bought a bit brighter pink and got away with that too. So, of course, I kept pushing the envelope, as they call it these days. When I got to bright red, the teacher—who later went on to quite an illustrious career in educational administration—told me I had gone too far. I had better come to school with a lighter shade tomorrow.

So, what did I do? I put on a darker shade, of course! Mr. Geraty was waiting for me at the door. When he saw what I had done, he took me by the hand and led me to the chemistry lab. He knew his chemistry well enough to know just how to take that polish off. This

Chapter Two

made me furious. The whole class was watching and snickering. I went home that night at least partly humbled, with a note from him to my mother. Mom was always very understanding—of the teacher's side of things, that is. At least that's the way it seemed to me. But I do have to admit that she was usually right. She seemed to have a way of knowing when I was telling the truth and when I was trying to pull the wool over her eyes, and she would defend me if she knew I was telling the truth. But all too often she had to add her punishment to whatever discipline I had received at school.

Mom tried very hard to raise Stan and me right, but she often had to work two jobs just to make ends meet, so we didn't see a lot of her. I usually tell people I was raised by notes. There would be a note by the stove, "Lentils in the fridge, have those for supper," or a note by the door, "Be sure to do all the dusting after school today."

Other than that, Stan and I were pretty much on our own, and we worked out a sort of silent pact between us that we wouldn't squeal on each other. Looking back on that, I realize that this agreement could have been a formula for disaster, especially since I had such an independent spirit. After that experience with Mr. Geraty in eighth grade, I decided that church school wasn't for me. I guess I was quite a brat. I just didn't like so many rules, so I persuaded Mom to let me go to public high school.

It didn't take me long to find the wrong crowd to run around with! One of my girlfriends bragged to me about how easy it was to sneak out of Woolworth's with a couple lipsticks or nail polish bottles in your pocket, so I decided I'd give it a try myself. I felt pretty cocky when I walked out of the store with two "free" lipsticks secreted away in my purse. But all my bravado vanished when I felt a hand with a firm grip on my shoulder.

I turned around and stared into the face of a hard-looking policewoman. The image is still indelibly etched in my memory, more than half a century later. I even remember that she was wearing a purple blouse made of some sort of shiny see-through material. I could guess from the way she was holding onto me that she wasn't going to let go. She took me back into the store and marched me up to her office, a tiny, stuffy place about the size of a closet, and sat me down.

Then she took my purse and turned it upside down, dumping out everything, including the pilfered merchandise.

I was so ashamed I was in tears. What were they going to do with me? Throw me in jail? Send me to Alcatraz? "Miss, what you have done is a serious crime," the lady announced. "Now, I suggest you give me your name, address, and telephone number. One of our police officers will be paying a visit to your parents this evening."

That was almost worse than a one-way trip to Alcatraz! I knew how disappointed my mother would be. I had shamed and dishonored her. But there was nothing I could do, so I gave the required information.

I don't think the police ever actually came by our house, but I was so afraid that they would that I spilled the whole story myself. I'll never forget the look on my mother's face when she said, "And to think I've raised a thief!" I was thoroughly shamed and ashamed, and looking back on the experience, I thank God that I got caught. The scare that policewoman gave me ended my career in crime. I can honestly say I've never stolen so much as a bobby pin since that day!

Mom was still very busy with all the work she had to do just to make ends meet, so Stan took it upon himself to keep a sharper eye on my activities. He was almost five years older than I, and his heart was in the right place, but I often wished he would loosen up a bit in his attempts to keep me out of mischief. The main trouble was that tactfulness was not one of his primary virtues.

But I guess he did have reason to be concerned about me. After all, I had started my romantic career pretty early in life. In fact, I remember getting in trouble once in the fifth grade for kissing a boy in school—well, of course, he started it! By the time I was sixteen, I was dating pretty regularly, going to dances, the theater, and big band performances. Oh, how I loved the music! I think I could sing every popular song from memory. But I never was much of a dancer.

When I was sixteen I caught the eye of a suave, sophisticated charmer of a fellow who was quite a bit older than me—twenty-six to be exact. Buck was one of those sweet-talking fellows who seemed so nice that even my mother didn't see anything wrong with my dating him. But Stan wasn't so sure. He did a little checking around and found out that Buck didn't exactly have a pristine reputation. One night when I came in after a date, Stan heard me coming up the steps onto the porch by his bedroom and pulled me aside. "I don't want you ever going out with that guy again," he said sternly.

"Oh, leave me alone," I responded curtly, pulling away from him. "What business is it of yours who I date?"

"Del," Stan said. "I'm serious. I've talked to some of this guy's friends, and you don't want to hear the kinds of stories they told me about him. I'm just going to warn you. Stay away from him. He's the kind of guy who slips things into girls' drinks, if you know what I mean. I don't want you going out with him again. I just won't hear of it. You understand? Now, if you'll agree to drop him, I won't say anything about this to Mother. But . . ."

His eyes said the rest of the sentence for him, and I knew that my days of dating Buck were over.

I suppose I was a bit naive in my relationship with Buck, but Mom had done a good job of teaching both Stan and me to have standards. I used to love the movies—of course they were a bit more innocent than most of what's out there today—and I was thrilled when I got a job as an usherette at a theater in downtown Oakland. It didn't take me long to figure out, though, that most of the girls who worked there were pretty loose. They'd brag about their latest affairs, each one trying to top the other.

And the manager of the place wasn't above taking advantage of their lack of morals. He must have thought of me as a pretty tough nut to crack, though. Finally he promoted me from usherette to cashier—partly because it gave him more of a chance to work on me, I think. I remember one day in particular when he came into the little office where we collected money for tickets and started talking to me. At first he was real nice—interested in how things were going for my family and that kind of thing—but after a few minutes he started saying suggestive things and using some pretty foul language. After this had gone on for a few minutes, I picked up my purse and said, "Excuse me," and headed out the door.

"What's the matter, are you sick? You got to go to the can?" he asked.

"No," I replied.

"There's a line of people here. You can't leave!" he said.

"Watch me," I said.

"Well, what's a matter with you?" he asked.

I said, "I'm not used to foul language like that. I don't have to take it. I don't need a job that bad."

"Oh, sit down, Del," he said. "I won't use language like that around you anymore."

It wasn't that I was a saint or anything like that, but I hadn't been raised in the gutter. And I let him know it, and he respected me for it. Maybe that's why I didn't appreciate Stan's forcefulness in telling me to stop dating Buck. I thought I could pretty well take care of myself, thank you very much!

After all, a girl just wants to have a little fun. And it wasn't until later that I found out about another time that my sibling guardian had intervened to protect me from myself. I think if I had known about it at the time, I would have throttled him.

Chapter Three

The one thing I wanted more than anything else as a teenager was to be a singer with a dance band. I loved hearing big bands play and really admired the women like Peggy Lee and Jo Stafford, who sang with them. That would be my dream vocation, I thought.

But for the time being I had to content myself with singing for my own amusement. I've always had a bit of stage fright—even to-day after singing in public for most of my life, I can get a case of the jitters when I have to do something out of the ordinary. But back then, it was far worse. I was afraid that if I ever had to sing on stage, I'd just collapse in a puddle of tears. So I would usually sing only when I was alone. But sing I did—while I was doing the dishes, while I was sweeping the floor, I'd even sing quietly while I was walking down the sidewalk. I started babysitting when I was nine years old, and sometimes I would sing to the kids I was taking care of, but that was the biggest audience I could handle. Both Stan and I had to take on jobs pretty early to help out with our school expenses. I would clean other people's houses for them—a good opportunity to sing, if no one was around. And dog sitting is another job I remember, but I'm not sure I ever sang to my canine charges. Of course the best place to sing and hear yourself is in the bathroom, where the sound bounces back off the walls all around you.

That's what I was doing one evening when Stan's best friend, Ed Harris, came over to visit. Stan and Ed were like brothers—Ed was just like one of the family. He would drop by our house anytime day or night, and if the door was open, he would just walk right in.

Well, that evening, when I was about seventeen or eighteen, I was home all alone and getting ready to go out for the evening, so I went into the bathroom and drew a bath. The warm water felt so good that I just sat back and relaxed for a bit and began to sing. I was singing so loud that I didn't hear the front door open or hear Stan and Ed come into the house. "Who's that singing?" Ed asked. "That's not Del, is it?"

"I don't know who else it would be," Stan answered.

"She's good!" Ed said. "I mean she's really good!"

"Ah, it's just Del, for heaven's sake," Stan said. "Haven't you ever heard her sing before?"

"Not like that! She's so good she could sing with a band, don't you think?"

"I don't know," Stan said.

"I do!" Ed said. "I know talent when I hear it. Hey, you know Stan Kenton and his band are going to be in town in a couple weeks. I know one of the guys that travels with him. You think maybe I ought to have him drop by and hear Del sing?"

Now, for those of you who didn't grow up on big band music, I ought to tell you that Stan Kenton's band was one of the hottest things going in those days. He probably wasn't as famous as Tommy Dorsey or Glen Miller, but he was well known. I've heard that Frank Sinatra even called him "the most significant figure of the Modern Jazz age."

My brother Stan and Ed were both quite musical themselves. Stan had played steel guitar with a few bands around Oakland, so he knew a bit about the music business and what went on backstage with some of the women who sang with bands. He looked Ed right in the eye and said, "Ed, don't you dare do that!"

"Why not?" Ed said. "Del's good. She's got talent. Maybe Kenton could give her a break—help her get a start in show business. Don't you think she'd like that?"

"Whether she'd like it or not is none of your business," Stan replied. "I said 'don't you dare do that,' and I meant it."

"Ah, come on. Don't be so protective," Ed said. "Del's a big girl. You ought to at least let her make her own decision. I'm going to suggest it to her."

"You do," Stan replied, "and you can consider our friendship ended. Don't ever darken the door of this place again. You understand?"

"Whoa! No offense intended, man," Ed said, raising his hands and backing off. "I can tell you're really serious about this, but don't you think Del ought to at least have a chance?"

"You heard what I said. And I meant it," Stan said. "Now, as far as I'm concerned, that's the end of the discussion. Don't ever bring it up again."

And he didn't.

I never even heard about the conversation until years later. If I had heard about it then, I would have been furious at Stan for squelching an opportunity like that!

But knowing what I know now, looking back on the way the Lord led in my life, I'm eternally grateful to my big brother for watching out for me.

I really did need all the help I could get to find my way through all the pitfalls of being raised by a single mother who had almost no time available to spend with her family. I can't say that I had a happy or idyllic childhood. I tried to cover the emptiness and discontent I felt inside with a brave exterior—I suppose many of my friends considered me the life of the party because I could crack jokes and make merry with the best of them. But deep down inside I knew there was something missing. And I'd often take it out on my poor, hard-working, longsuffering mother. I'd get so upset with her, and with Stan, too, for any restrictions they placed on my freedom, that I spent most of my teenage years looking forward to my eighteenth birthday—that would be liberation day for me, I declared.

When that day came, my mother had a little surprise in store for me. When I came home from work in the evening, she came out of the closet carrying a suitcase. "What's that for?" I asked. "Are you going on a trip?"

"No, it's for you," Mom replied.

"What for?" I asked, my heart skipping a beat. "Are you giving me a trip for my birthday?"

"No, it's your eighteenth birthday. I figured you'd be moving out, so I just wanted to help. Come on, we can put most of your things in here."

"Wha . . . Where will I go?"

"I assumed you had that all worked out by now. You've been telling me for years that you were moving out on your eighteenth birthday. I thought maybe I could rent out the room for a little extra cash."

"Oh, Mom! I didn't really mean it . . ."

"I figured you didn't." She snickered, stood up, and held open her arms. After she had hugged me, she reassured me. "You're welcome to stay here as long as you need to—and as long as you're willing to live according to a few simple rules. I want to help you get a good start in life."

But as I stepped into the pulpit that Sunday morning in the EUB church two years later, I didn't really think I needed much help at all. Though I was a bit jittery, I was ready to wow the people with my beautiful rendition of *Ave Maria* by Franz Schubert. For some reason, even though we were in a Protestant church, Bonnie had insisted that I sing the song in Latin.

The organist played the opening bars, and I launched into the song, right on cue: "*Ave Maria! Gratia plena Maria, gratia plena.*" It was really pretty easy for me to say the Latin words, and I continued on, singing my heart out, putting all my feelings into what I was sure was the most beautiful rendition of the song in anyone's memory.

I got so involved in the music, and so confident in my ability to remember the words, that I even forgot to turn the page. Page two ended with an *Ave Maria* that lasted for three bars, including a pause, and the song picked up on page three with another *Ave Maria*. I paused at the appropriate place at the end of the second page and looked out over the congregation, who were listening with rapt attention. It felt so good to see how they were being moved by the music!

Then it was time to pick up with page three. *"Ave Maria"* I sang, then looked down. I hadn't turned the page. What came next? I fumbled with the music, but couldn't get it open to the right place. The next words were *"Mater Dei, Ora pro nobis peccatoribus,"* but I couldn't find them anywhere on the paper, or in my memory.

Music can't wait. The organist played on, and I had to follow. "Mater poly sophis, Arta foly corbis," I sang. Making up Latin-sounding words as I went along. Fortunately I knew where each *Ave Maria* fit. And as long as I slotted all of those phrases in the right places, nobody knew the difference.

Except for our choir director, Bonnie. Fortunately she had sat down in the second row of the choir and was able to bend down and fiddle with the buckle on her shoe so that no one in the congregation saw how hard she was struggling to keep from bursting out laughing.

But boy did we have a good howl about it afterward!

Laughing was one of the things Bonnie did best. And I think that's the thing that attracted me to her when we first met. In fact, it was Bonnie's laughter, her *joie de vivre*—the pure joy she took in life itself—that would indirectly lead me away from the selfish life I was pursuing to one that held more joy than I could ever have imagined or brought about by following my own way.

Chapter Four

I met Bonnie when I went to work at Pacific Greyhound Lines in downtown Oakland. It was my first job out of high school—I'd worked part time at the theater for several years, but after graduation I knew I needed to get something full time and better paying. I still had dreams of being a professional singer with a dance band but realized that the opportunity probably wouldn't just jump out of the bushes and bite me. So I figured I ought to work and start saving up some money in hopes of getting to go to college some day.

Bonnie was the one who greeted me when I walked into the office to apply for the job of secretary to the assistant manager. Perky, full of fun, with blue eyes that just sparkled, she was a good choice for a receptionist. She made me feel welcome and ushered me right in to see the man I would be working for if I should get the job. A few days later she was the one who called to tell me that I should report to work the next day if I was still looking for a job. She called me "Miss Delker" that time—but it was the last time we'd be formal with each other.

We hit it off like a couple of twins separated at birth. We'd spend all day together at work, go to lunch together at a diner across the street (where the assistant manager would sometimes buy our lunch for us), and then go off somewhere together in the evening too.

Chapter Four

Just as Bonnie was perfectly suited for the job of receptionist, I found that the job I'd gotten was well suited to my talents. One of the responsibilities of my boss, A. W. Bobo, was to supervise the bus drivers and make sure they were doing a good job. Pacific Greyhound was very concerned about its reputation and didn't want its drivers doing anything unsafe or anything that would give the company a bad name. So they hired people to go out in cars and follow the buses, and other people to ride the buses to see how the drivers were doing. These "secret agents" would bring back a report, and the drivers would get demerits for anything they had done wrong. Too many demerits could lead to dismissal.

Mr. Bobo would collect the agents' reports and then write letters to the drivers, informing them of any problems that had been noted. He soon found out that I had a natural talent for correspondence, so it wasn't long before the bus drivers started getting letters written by a teenage girl who had never sat behind the wheel of a car, instructing them in how to drive. Of course, Mr. Bobo would sign the letters, so the drivers never knew it was me who was trying to straighten them out.

After a day of writing letters, answering phones, and other secretarial duties, Bonnie and I were ready for some fun. We loved music, dancing, and going on dates to the movie theater or to hear a dance band play, and that's how we would spend many of our weekends. But there was one thing I enjoyed that Bonnie would have no part of. Bonnie made no bones about the fact that her father was an alcoholic. And that had put the fear of the bottle in her. She didn't want to follow in his footsteps, so she was a confirmed teetotaler. If a beverage had alcohol in it, she wanted nothing to do with it.

Not me. It wasn't long after my eighteenth birthday that I started developing a real taste for beer, wine, and mixed drinks. Not that I'd drink myself under the table or anything like that, but the stuff just tasted good to me, and made me feel good too.

Mom was pretty concerned about that. She was a religious woman who had been baptized into the Seventh-day Adventist Church at age eighteen, after attending a series of evangelistic meetings at the invitation of some of her cousins. She had remained a faithful mem-

ber through the years and accepted the health and temperance teach-
ings of the Church, which called for total abstinence from such things
as smoking and drinking alcoholic beverages. She didn't have to worry
much about the possibility that I would take up smoking. I'd gotten
that out of my system when I was about fourteen and found a pack of
Pall Malls® cigarettes at a house where I was babysitting. I'd seen my
sophisticated Aunt Emma take long drags off cigarettes, so I figured
that was the proper way to smoke. I felt so cool! For a very short time.

When the couple returned after their date, they found me curled
up on the couch, a delicate shade of green. And I had little desire to
ever try cigarettes again.

Mother wanted me to be brought up right. She had worked extra
hard to scrape together enough money to send me to church-affili-
ated schools starting with the fifth grade, but as I mentioned before,
I'd had enough of that sort of thing. I wanted to be able to live my
life just the way I pleased. Looking back, I thank God for those years
in church school. Many good seeds were planted in my soul that
bore fruit later.

During my childhood and teen years, Mom continued to consider herself a church member, but by the time the weekend rolled
around, she was usually too tired to go to church.

As for me, I was just as happy not to be dragged to church every
week. There were so many interesting things to do in the world; why
would I want to take a whole day out just to worship God? And
since our church taught that the Sabbath began on Friday night at
sundown—well, that could really interfere with a girl's social life. I'd
decided religion was for older folks, not for a girl like me.

I didn't have a car, and neither did any of my friends, so one way
to get around was by bus. That was the way I got to and from work
every day. But there was a quicker way too. It was war time, and
there were lots of GI's around—soldiers, sailors, and marines—and
it was perfectly acceptable for a young fellow out on leave to just
stick out his thumb and hitch a ride. People driving by almost felt
like it was their patriotic duty to stop and give the fellow a lift.

One night one of my girlfriends and I had dates with a couple of
servicemen, and when they came and picked us up, we just went to

a bus stop and sat down on the bench. After a few minutes, one of the fellows stuck out his thumb. It wasn't long before a car stopped and the four of us piled into the back seat. The man giving us a ride was a Navy officer, and it soon became apparent that he had been partying already that night—and that he'd had a bit too much to drink. We squealed around corners and sped across the Oakland Bay Bridge, headed for a theater in downtown San Francisco, sometimes driving on the wrong side of the road. We pleaded with him to slow down, but it only seemed to make him angry, and he decided to show us just how fast he could go around a corner.

Unfortunately he was a bit too enthusiastic about his car's cornering ability. We went up on two wheels, and then came down with a crash that shattered glass on the right side of the car. The car skidded along on its side until we hit a power pole. I had been sitting on the right side of the back seat, and, of course, seat belts hadn't even been thought of in those days. The four of us ended up in a heap, with me at the bottom. No one was badly hurt, but all of us had bumps, scrapes, and bruises, and there was quite a bit of blood involved. All of which seemed to get on my white dress. Stan had gotten married a few years earlier, so Mom and I were living in a really small house at that time, with only one bedroom. When I got home, Mom woke up and wondered what all the blood was about. I was too shook up to talk about it just then. "I was in an accident. Can I tell you about it in the morning?" I pleaded.

Mom could see how troubled I was and wisely left me alone. Next morning, though, I had to tell her exactly what had happened. "I'm just thankful you're still alive!" she said.

She could have taken the opportunity to give me a lecture about the dangers of drinking and driving, but she didn't.

Mom wasn't the type to harp at me or nag me about my lifestyle, but she was very concerned. So she was really delighted when Bonnie and I hit it off so well. She was always glad when I'd go on a group date with my friend from work, because she knew there wouldn't be any drinking involved.

Bonnie loved music just as much as I did, but she had no aspirations of singing with a dance band. She found her outlet at church, and it wasn't long before she got me involved in the choir she had begun directing when she was eighteen years old—about the time I met her. The women from the choir also formed an ensemble that would take appointments at the United Service Organizations Club (USO) and other places to do secular music. I think it was Thursday nights that were reserved for ensemble practice at the church, and Bonnie and I soon found a bar right near one of the bus stops along our way, where you could get a full steak dinner for $1.25. No doubt the proprietor offered the dinner discount in hopes of getting people to come in and order some drinks to go with it, but since I was with Bonnie, we always just ate dinner and went merrily on our way. The bartender never complained, but he and some of his customers seemed to find our behavior rather amusing.

For the most part we were just a couple of happy-go-lucky single girls in a city full of fellows who'd been called away from home to serve their country. We had some great times together, but I soon learned that going on a double date with Bonnie could be a bit problematic. She didn't like going out with a fellow alone on the first date, so she'd usually ask if he had a buddy. Then she'd call me up and ask if I wanted to date the fellow's friend.

I said Yes the first few times. But I soon figured out that I usually got the short end of the stick. *Why was it that the handsome, suave, charming fellows she met always had such duds for friends?* I wondered. It wasn't long before I had become pretty gun shy. When she'd call me up and ask me to accompany her on a date I'd just say, "Oh, found another drip for me, huh?" and let her find someone else to go along.

I was ready to do that again one Saturday afternoon when she called up. But that particular time, Mom intervened. And for once I ended up being glad she did.

Chapter Five

The fighting of World War II ended when Japan surrendered on August 15, 1945. Two-and-a-half weeks later, Japanese representatives signed the surrender documents on the deck of the battleship, USS *Missouri,* and the war was officially over.

Bonnie and I hadn't been directly involved in the war effort, except when our singing group entertained at the USO. And, of course, we did our share to keep some of the servicemen entertained on Friday and Saturday nights as well. The end of the war didn't mean that our patriotic responsibilities in that area suddenly came to an end. San Francisco was, after all, one of the world's busiest military ports and always had a ready supply of sailors and marines.

The two of us gals continued to enjoy good, harmless fun with a wide variety of dates. Neither of us was much in the mood for settling down and starting a family yet, so we never let relationships get very serious.

Bonnie dated more than I did, I suppose because she was more outgoing, and she had the added advantage of having three good-looking sisters. Of course my decision not to accept most of the dates she offered me also contributed to a few lonely evenings on my part.

So it was with mixed emotions that I listened to her plea when she called up that Saturday afternoon. "Del, you've got to help me out," she said.

"What is it now?" I asked, lightheartedly.

"Wanda was downtown today and saw four marines on a street corner."

"Yes," I said, already knowing where this was going and what my answer would be. Wanda was outgoing and attractive, so I didn't have any trouble imagining what the marines' response would be.

"Well, they whistled at her, and she went over and started talking to them. And guess what?"

"They're all there right now, and there's one that needs a date—probably a real drip if I don't miss my guess," I responded,

"No, Del, this one's really nice. You'll like him. I know it. We've got three girls to go on a date, but this poor fellow—he was injured in the war, for heaven's sake—just got out of the hospital, but he's doing great. Come on, Del. Just this once? I promise you—you'll have a great time with him."

"No thanks," I said. "This isn't quite the first time you've told me you found a great date for me, Bonnie. I think I'll find my own men from here on out, thank you just the same."

There wasn't much privacy in the tiny home I shared with my mother. Mom quickly caught on to what was going on and joined in the conversation from across the room, saying how nice it would be for me to go out on a date with Bonnie again. Now I was getting stereophonic pleading, and this was in the days before even hi-fi had been invented!

Finally I gave in. "You'd better be right about this one," I told Bonnie. "Or you know for sure I'll never go on a blind date with you again."

"He is different. He's really sweet, and he's seen your picture and wants to meet you," she assured me. So I hung up and got ready for what I hoped (but doubted) would be a fun date with four marines.

Boy was I in for a surprise! Bob Thompson, the young marine from Ohio that Bonnie had set me up with, turned out to be one of the most fun and nicest guys I had ever dated. And he was handsome too! I don't remember where we went on that first date, most likely to a movie, but when the evening was over, Bob asked if he could have permission to call me again sometime. I pretended to think about it for a minute, but then scribbled my phone number on a scrap of paper and gave it to him.

It turned out to be one of the smartest things I'd ever done. Not that Bob and I became any great romantic duo or anything, but we really enjoyed each others' company, and enjoyed doing a lot of things together over the next several weeks—until Bob started bugging me about something.

He wanted me to go somewhere that I had no interest in at all. I was Thoroughly Modern Del and didn't want religion interfering with the fun I was having. Sure, I still went with Bonnie to church occasionally and sang in the choir, and sometimes I'd go with Mom to church, too. But that was about as much religion as I could handle. Bonnie's church was quite evangelistic in nature, and often the Sunday service would end with a call for people to come down to the front and give their hearts to Jesus. I can remember more than once being the only one still seated in the choir loft. In fact; I was probably the only one still seated in the whole church. Everyone else was down with the preacher, giving their hearts to the Lord all over again.

It wasn't that I was against religion. In fact, I suppose that the real reason I didn't respond to those calls was that I took them very seriously. I didn't think a person should go down to the altar and weep and pray just because everyone else was doing it. I wasn't about to make a show of commitment to something unless I really meant it.

Bob was probably more religiously inclined than I. He had served as a chaplain's assistant during the war. While he was in the hospital, his mother had come out from Ohio to visit him and had just been wandering around downtown Oakland one day when she'd noticed the words "The Quiet Hour" on a sign on the front of a building. Curious, she went over to have a closer look and discovered that it was the headquarters of a religious radio broadcast. Wanting to know more, she went inside and was surprised by the warmth of the reception she received. At that time The Quiet Hour, which had been founded by Pastor J. L. Tucker in 1937, had a bookstore and a chapel where they held evangelistic meetings regularly, and Bob's mother was quite intrigued. She went back to the hospital and told Bob all about it. He was being treated for battle fatigue (what we call post-traumatic stress disorder today) as a result of witnessing some terrible atrocities in China. She thought maybe the folks at The Quiet Hour could help him, so she took him by for a visit as soon as he got out of the hospital.

No sooner was he inside the door than Eugene Erickson, J. L. Tucker's son-in-law, greeted him. Eugene took him for a tour of the facilities and invited him to come back in the evening when there would be a meeting.

Bob attended meetings a few times, and soon after we started dating, he began urging me to go there for a visit too.

"What's the name of the program?" I asked absently, not really interested. "The Quiet Hour," he said.

"The Quiet Hour?" I asked. "You're kidding! What a boring sounding name!" Meditation wasn't in my vocabulary. I couldn't think of anything less interesting than quiet. Now, if he'd invited me to go to a place called "The Noisy Hour"—well, that would have been different! I'd have probably dropped everything to go.

"No, really. It's a neat place," Bob said. "You ought to go there with me sometime!"

"No thanks," I said. "I think I'll pass on that."

The next day at work I laughingly told Bonnie all about it. We both had a giggle over the name of the place and agreed it wasn't the kind of entertainment we were looking for. But the next time I saw Bob, guess what he wanted to talk about?

I complained to Bonnie about it the following day. "The guy's got a one-track mind," I said. "All he can talk about is Quiet Hour, Quiet Hour. He's not going to let me alone until I go there with him!"

"Well, would it really be so bad?" Bonnie asked. "I mean, here's a guy who's risked his life to defend our country. Maybe you ought to go with him just once—just to kind of thank him for what he's done."

Chapter Five

"Oh, so now it's my patriotic duty to go?" I asked.

"Well, not really. But what have you got to lose—I mean it sounds like the people there must be really nice. How bad can it be? And besides, a little religion might not hurt you a bit! Come on, let's go tonight. I'll get my sister to come along too, and we can have a good time together."

With Bonnie's change of attitude, I was out of allies. Mom, too, had suggested that maybe it wouldn't be such a bad idea for me to visit the radio studios with Bob. What she knew and I didn't was that The Quiet Hour was sponsored by Seventh-day Adventists— her own denomination. She had gone to the EUB church with me once to hear me sing. But all the while she'd been praying that some day my voice could be used to glorify God within the denomination she had brought me up in.

"Oh, all right. I'll go, I guess," I said. "But just once. And just for Bob's sake. I don't need a bunch of religious people telling me what I can and can't do!" Religion was all rules and regulations. And the fewer of those I had in my life, the happier I would be—or so I thought.

Chapter Six

Bob, Wanda, Bonnie, and I arrived at The Quiet Hour that evening. The other three seemed quite excited to be going to a place where they produced a religious radio broadcast, but I was anything but enthusiastic. In fact, I think I went with a chip on my shoulder and my nose curled up. I just wanted to get it over with and head out to do something more interesting.

At the door to greet us was Eugene Erickson and his wife, Jewel. They were so sweet and nice to us, taking us on a tour and inviting us to the evening's meeting, that I found myself smiling in spite of myself.

"Well, what did you think?" Bob asked on the way home. "Was that so bad?"

"No, I guess not," I responded. I wouldn't give him the satisfaction of telling him how warm and happy the place had made me feel. And maybe that's why he never insisted that I go back with him. I think he visited The Quiet Hour several more times before he was discharged and sent home to Ohio. I talked to him recently and learned that still today, even though he and his wife have had health problems, they give of themselves to bless others by providing transportation for those in need and helping elderly folks. They are dedicated Christians.

Chapter Six

I guess you wouldn't call our time together a real romance. Bob and I had become good friends, but never with any great thoughts about the future. Still, when he was gone, it left me feeling a little lonely for a while. Most people know that I've never married, and I suppose some think that I never had a romantic thought in my life, never intended to settle down with a man and raise a family. Nothing could be further from the truth. I really enjoyed the dating scene when I was young, and even though I mainly played the field, I always believed that someday just the right man would come along and sweep me off my feet.

Maybe I was lonely, or just sentimental, but somehow I found my way back to The Quiet Hour one evening, all by myself. As soon as I slipped in the door, there were Eugene and Jewel to greet me. It was almost like they'd just been waiting for me to come back, and soon I felt that same warm feeling that had come over me the first time. It was kind of like coming home.

I attended the meeting that night and started going back for meetings every once in a while. Then one evening Pastor J. L. Tucker preached about heaven. Oh, how that man could paint word pictures! He described the beautiful flowers that would bloom year-round, and the animals—how we'd be able to pet wolves and lions and tigers—and the beautiful birds that would fly right up and eat out of our hands. Then he talked about getting to meet Abraham and David and other great patriarchs, and meeting our ancestors and people we'd known who had passed to their rest. He said he wanted to be able to talk to his guardian angel and find out all the different times his life had been spared or he'd been protected from temptation.

Then he talked about meeting Jesus and looking into His loving eyes and being able to sit down and talk with our Savior. It seemed like Pastor Tucker was looking right at me when he asked, "I want to be there, don't you? I want to see Jesus. I want to live with Him for all eternity. Don't you?"

He didn't make a call, didn't invite those who wanted to be in heaven to come forward for prayer, or anything like that. But his words moved me just the same. I couldn't get that picture of heaven

31

out of my mind. I knew I wanted to be there. It seemed like my whole attitude toward religion changed in that one moment. I knew now that I wanted to be a Christian—that I really wanted to be in heaven.

I went home, feeling like I was walking on a cloud. But then in the morning when I got up and started to put on my makeup, things seemed a little different. "I guess I won't be able to use this any-more," I said, looking at my rouge and mascara. "Maybe this religion thing isn't for me, after all." Perhaps I was convinced, but not con-verted. The devil doesn't give up easily! I'd come to think of religion as just a bunch of rules. A story that was often told in our family concerned a couple of my aunts, who had been coaxed into going to church with my mother one day. When the preacher saw them come in, loaded with makeup and jewelry, he suddenly switched the topic of his sermon and went on and on for the next half hour about how evil it was to get a "premadie"—he meant permanent, but appar-ently couldn't say the word right. He'd decided he needed to preach directly at the "sins" of the ladies who had come to visit. Back in the 1920s, getting a permanent wave in your hair was a new thing and considered quite risqué, but my aunts weren't at all impressed with the preacher's reasoning and almost never darkened the door of the church again. As long as they lived, they enjoyed laughing about the preacher's "premadies."

That kind of religion didn't appeal to me at all. And all I could think about for the next couple of days was all the things I enjoyed that I would have to give up if I "got religion." But then as I was going to sleep one night, Pastor Tucker's words came back into my mind, and I saw the beautiful scene he had painted all over again, and knew I just had to be there. Maybe I could give up a few of my worldly pleasures for the joy of spending eternity with Jesus. Maybe it wasn't too much to ask. But just how much did I have to give up? Could I strike some sort of bargain with God and be able to at least put on just enough makeup to make me look nice?

I decided I had to know. I had to make a decision, right away, as to whether I wanted to go to heaven, or whether I wanted to enjoy life on earth, doing things my own way. So the next time I went to

I was about nine months old when my picture was first taken. This was one of the last times I willingly let someone push me around.

With Mom at my third birthday party—shortly before my first professional singing gig.

Here I am at age twelve.

Aren't we cute? Brother Stan's about thirteen, I'm about nine here.

Me with an attitude—a few years later.

Stan as a young boy—are those
South Dakota bib overalls?

In 1943 Stan joined the Army Air Force
and soon shipped out to England.

Stan flew many missions with a bomber squadron in Europe. He escaped
serious injury, but a bullet went through his helmet once.

Stan and his wife, Claire

One of my happiest days was the day Stan
was baptized in 1968.

Dennis, Stan's younger son, and his wife, Irene. Dennis resisted the Lord for many years but now he often shows up at my place with a Bible under his arm.

Joey Delker, my nephew, earned a Ph.D. at Loma Linda University, but died young of multiple sclerosis.

My half-sister Laverne and my half-brother Harry are the people in the middle in this picture. I've only gotten well acquainted with them in recent years. Laverne has helped me better understand and love my father, whom I previously knew only from negative stories about his treatment of my mother.

Here's the group that was together the night we rode with a drunk naval officer and ended up in a car accident. I thank the Lord for preserving me through many foolhardy adventures before I came to really know and accept Him.

My mother was a patient, hardworking, and very creative woman who urged me to stop acting like Jonah!

All decked out—must be ready for another date?

One of my first professional photos after I began singing at VOP.

The house where I rented a room when I first joined VOP.

I wish I could still do this—probably taken during college days.

Here's something I can still do—touch my nose with my tongue—and I've made lots of friends—especially young people—by taking time to have fun with them. Rob Truscott can do it too!

In 1953 I began my college studies at Emanuel Missionary College, where I was delighted to get acquainted with Minerva Constantine, whose whole family was baptized through the influence of VOP.

The next year I went to La Sierra College. This picture was printed in VOP News along with a news note about my studies.

This is my senior picture, taken in 1958.

Mom and me on graduation day.

When I went to college at La Sierra, starting in 1954, Sonja Rust was my roommate.

I still talk to Sonja regularly and visit her—and her cat—when I get a chance.

A couple more pictures of me from about the time I went away to college. The left one was actually done in color!

In the beginning I often sang five-part numbers with the quartet, or duets with one of the members. But soon we started doing multiple recordings in which I would sing up to four parts myself. One lady wrote in and said, "I like Del Delker, but I don't like the girls singing with her!" Someone took the time to hand cut and paste these three pictures together to publicize my multiple recordings.

The star-studded production where I played Ellen White and Jack Veazey played James never made it to Broadway. But this was taken in Las Vegas.

Not many people know that I was also a television star. The VOP News reported in 1951 that our staff had made some television programs, and that I had a starring role in one of them!

Elmer Walde, shown here reviewing scripts with The Chief, was the announcer on the broadcast in the early 1950s. He played an important role in keeping me from getting discouraged and leaving VOP.

The new building that VOP moved into in 1950.

The entire staff posed for a picture on the front steps in 1961.

Here are a few more pictures from my early days with VOP.
I was sure dark colors were best for a
serious gospel singer—and beware of too much smiling!

Enough about me for a while—here are some pictures of a few of my friends.

Here's Bob Thompson, the U. S. Marine that Bonnie introduced me to. He's the one who insisted I visit The Quiet Hour. I'm eternally grateful to him for that!

Bonnie Barnett—my best buddy from the Greyhound office. Isn't she pretty?

Bob and Carol Thompson, just a few years ago. Despite failing health they're still active in helping others.

Pastor J. L. Tucker of The Quiet Hour taught me about heaven and led me to Jesus.

Boleslaw Fries, world's smartest cat. It's too bad you can't see her colors—she was a beautiful calico.

Two of the most important and dearest people in my life. H. M. S. Richards (The Chief) and his dear wife, Mabel.

The Chief and Mabel's sons Kenneth (far left) and Harold eventually joined their father at VOP. Here they pose with their wives, Jackie and Mary, and mother, Mabel. Joining them are Lonnie Melashenko, current director-speaker of VOP, and his wife, Jeannie.

This is the group I first made music with at VOP. From the left, organist Al Avila, second tenor Bob Seamount, bass Jerry Dill, myself, baritone Wayne Hooper, and first tenor Bob Edwards. This King's Heralds group sang together on the broadcast from 1949 until 1961.

Harold and his father were VOP's broadcast team for more than 20 years.

Mabel recently celebrated her 103rd birthday! This photo was snapped when some of her friends gathered in honor of birthday number 101.

I've had the privilege of traveling with many different accompanists through the years—and they all remained my friends!

Beth Thurston accompanied me at meetings in the early '50s. She's the one who encouraged me to be more outgoing and friendly with the audience.

Brad Braley was my main accompanist for nineteen years. He could coax beautiful music out of almost any instrument with a keyboard.

Brad's wife, Olive, usually traveled with us. They often performed keyboard duets, and she was also in demand for her dramatic readings.

Wilma Boting was another of my early accompanists.

Calvin Taylor began accompanying me in 1972 and traveled regularly with me after Brad retired.

At age twenty-five, Jim Teel became my accompanist—during my thirtieth year with VOP.

Hugh Martin, composer of "Have Yourself a Merry Little Christmas," traveled to camp meetings with me for four summers. Audiences loved listening to his music as well as his testimony telling how he became a Christian.

Janice Wright and I made only a few trips together in the 1980s, but we enjoyed every one!

Fernando "Ferdie" Westre worked extensively with our Spanish broadcast, and also accompanied me on several trips.

Phil Draper first accompanied me when I went with Harold Richards to Australia and New Zealand in 1986. He still accompanies me regularly sixteen years later.

Jim, Ferdie, Phil, and Hugh were able to join me when we taped the Del and Friends video in 2002.

The Quiet Hour studios, I asked if I could have an appointment with Pastor Tucker. He was such a kind man and absolutely delighted to take some time with me.

That was how I found myself seated in his office, across the desk from him, ready to ask the most important question of my life. I began by telling him how much I appreciated his ministry and how I had really enjoyed his sermon about heaven.

He graciously thanked me for my kind words, and then I came right out with it. "Pastor Tucker," I said, "I really, really want to go to heaven."

"You certainly can, Del," he responded. "Just accept Jesus as your Savior and be baptized in His name."

"It's not quite that easy," I countered, getting right to the point. "What I want to know is, what do I have to give up?"

My question caught him by surprise, and he looked puzzled for a moment, then suddenly the light seemed to dawn. He could see that I liked to wear a little makeup and that my dresses sometimes wouldn't pass muster with some of the saints at church, and he understood what I was asking.

I still remember how he reacted. He had a big swivel chair, and he leaned way back and kind of chuckled, then laughed right out loud. Then he looked at me and smiled so I would know he wasn't laughing at me. "That's a very good question, Del," he said. "You want to know what you have to give up in order to get into heaven?"

"That's right," I said, wondering what he found so funny about it. I was dead serious. I had to decide whether it was worth it to live for Jesus or not.

"I'll tell you what, Del," he said. "I know there's a lot of people in the church who have whole long lists of what you can and can't do if you want to be a Christian—and what you can and can't wear. But I prefer to keep it simple. Here's what I'd say about how you look: If you can walk out of the house without drawing undue attention to yourself, you'll be on the right track."

The simplicity of his answer astounded me. I had expected a set of rules—something like the church school had had. I wanted to know just how dark of nail polish was OK, and whether or not I could wear a little mascara, and what colors of dresses were all right, and how tight was too tight when it came to skirts. But instead of all that, he had given me a simple principle that made infinitely more sense. If I was going to be a Christian, I ought not to be drawing attention to myself. I ought to be pointing people to Jesus instead.

We talked for a long while after that, with Pastor Tucker encouraging me to fully give my heart to the Lord and let Jesus work out the rest of the details. But the main thing I remember is the simplicity of that one answer. It's stayed with me all these years, and I've often used it in counseling other women who had a problem with church standards.

The lighter-than-air feeling had returned after my talk with the pastor, and it seemed like I could walk on clouds again. I was falling in love with Jesus, and my life was changing in ways I would never have dreamed possible.

Suddenly religion wasn't just a bunch of rules and regulations. It was about loving God and letting God's love flow through me to other people. And as for the rules—well, the Holy Spirit could take care of that end of the bargain. He was convicting me about changes that needed to be made in my life. Surely He could do the same for others. It wasn't my job to go around telling people what they could and couldn't do. My job was simply to point them to Jesus and let Him do the rest.

I never dreamed at that time, though, how much my life would change, or how much of my time would be devoted to doing that very thing—pointing people to the love of God as revealed in our Savior Jesus Christ.

Chapter Seven

The love of God would become the theme of my life—and soon it would be my theme song as well. But there were a few things that needed to be worked out first.

I continued to go to meetings at The Quiet Hour every time I got a chance. I was so thrilled with the things I was learning that I urged Bonnie to come and listen too, and she did a few times, but she was very happy in the church she belonged to and didn't want to make any changes. She did agree to invite her pastor to meet my pastor and see if the two of them couldn't come to some sort of agreement about what the truth was. The meeting didn't prove particularly fruitful, I'm afraid. I think the two pastors just agreed to disagree, and on the issue of religion, Bonnie and I came to about the same conclusion. We continued to be good friends, but she went to her church and I went to mine.

Music continued to be an important part of both of our lives. Now, fifty-five years later, I continue to sing solos for church gatherings (although I've never had another opportunity to sing *Ave Maria* in public!), and Bonnie has just recently retired from directing a large choir at a church and taken on responsibility for a smaller group.

After attending meetings at The Quiet Hour for several months, I finally made the decision to be baptized and join the Church. Conversion is an ongoing, growing process. I believe I was converted the night

I heard the sermon about heaven. That's when the seed was planted. From that night on I knew that I wanted to be a Christian. But I still had a lot of growing to do. I wasn't quite ready to give everything in my life over into God's care yet. There were questions about lifestyle, but those soon evaporated under the loving instruction of my new friends. And there was a bit of a problem at Pacific Greyhound when I announced that I was going to start attending church on Saturday instead of coming to work. My boss threatened to fire me, but I guess he liked what I did well enough that he finally agreed to work things out so that I could work just Monday through Friday.

It didn't take long for Pastor Tucker to discover that I had some talent for music. The Quiet Hour had a daily live radio broadcast in those days, and once in a while they'd have Jewel, Bonnie, and I, sing a trio.

It was in March 1947 that I took my stand to be baptized and join the Church. The day of my baptism, March 27, Pastor Tucker took me aside and sat down with me. He told me how delighted he was that I had chosen to be baptized; then he looked at me with a very serious expression on his face. "You know, Del," he said. "You're joining a perfect message. The message of Jesus and His love is just exactly what the world needs to hear."

I nodded my head in agreement; then he continued. "But always remember one thing, and this is very important. The people who are God's messengers aren't perfect. The people who bear the message are not the message. They are flawed human beings. So don't ever look at the people and criticize them and get discouraged. Don't ever say, 'Well, so and so did such and such, and because of that I'm leaving the church.' Continue to look to Jesus. He's the only One who's perfect."

That was precious advice. I've always remembered it, and it has helped me get through a lot of rough spots that otherwise might have made me stumble and lose sight of my Savior. Unfortunately, I've had the opportunity to see the negative side of things in God's work more often than I would have liked. I've known leaders in the Church who lost sight of Jesus and went astray. There have even been times when I thought that some people in leadership had about as much foresight as a grasshopper, jumping and bashing his head against a wall. But through it all, Pastor Tucker's advice has helped me keep on an even keel most of the time. It's not my responsibility to straighten out all the people in the world, or even in the church. That's the Holy Spirit's work. What I need to do is be sure that I keep my life focused on Jesus so that others can see Him through me.

I think it was my first pastor's example and counsel that made God's love such an important part of my belief and my ministry. I know that when I first heard the song "The Love of God," it struck a resonant chord in my heart, and I knew I needed to learn to sing it.

But even that decision wasn't without its pitfalls.

Within a month after my baptism I had a phone call one day from the man who was making arrangements for musicians to take part in a large Christian camp meeting to be held in Lodi, seventy miles east of Oakland, the second week of June. He had heard of me through people at The Quiet Hour and wondered whether I would be willing to sing a solo.

Of course my answer was Yes. But the closer I got to the date that had been set, the more nervous I felt. Why had I ever agreed to such a thing? Singing in front of Bonnie's church or singing at The Quiet Hour, where I knew most of the people, wasn't hard. Even singing on the radio, where I didn't have to look at the audience, was something I could handle. But this? Singing in front of several thousand strangers? My knees shook at the thought of it, and more than once I almost decided to call the man back and tell him I wouldn't be able to come.

But then, hadn't it always been my dream to sing in front of a large audience? Of course, now I wouldn't be singing for my own glory. It would all be for God's glory. But still it felt good. People were beginning to recognize that I had talent, and surely there was nothing wrong with feeling a little bit proud of the ability God had given to me.

The anticipation began to build up inside me. When the day finally arrived and I rode into the Lodi campground with some of my friends from The Quiet Hour, I went to the large auditorium where the meetings were held as soon as I could and looked over the platform. My heart swelled with pride as I realized that something very big was about to happen in my life. Finally I'd have the chance I had always dreamed of. Maybe if things went well enough, I could even become a professional singer. I sank down onto one of the wooden benches near the platform and let my imagination run wild.

When the time came for me to actually sing, though, I felt quite different. *How had I ever gotten myself into this?* I wondered. I just knew I was going to walk out onto the stage, trip, fall down, break an arm, and have to be hauled to the hospital in an ambulance. Or, what could be even worse, I'd forget my lines or lose my place, and this time I'd be singing in English and there'd be no chance to fake it.

But I'd made the commitment, and there was no backing out now. I walked out to the pulpit and made it there without tripping. There must have been 3,000 eager faces waiting to hear me, but they were all a blur to me.

The organist played the opening chords of the song I had chosen: "The Love of God," and when she got to the place where I was to sing, I opened my mouth and the words came out. The right words! On tune! And at the right time! And I made it all the way through the song without fainting. At the end of the last chorus, as the organ music faded away, the crowd was an enthusiastic sea of Amens! When I walked off the platform, I was immediately greeted by people who were waiting backstage to do their part in the program, and several of them shook my hand warmly and told me how much the song had blessed them. And after the meeting many others came to the front, just to tell me how much they had enjoyed my singing.

I was on cloud nine—for a few minutes. Yes, I had finally arrived, and I had proven that I could sing in front of a crowd. And people had recognized my talent. I couldn't imagine that I could ever feel happier or more blessed.

But when all the fuss was over and it was time to go back to the little rented room where I would be spending the next few days as I attended camp meeting, suddenly a very different feeling came over me.

My baptism day was only a couple of months behind me, and ever since that day when I had given my life totally into God's keeping, I had experienced a feeling of peace and contentment like I had never known before. My teenage years had been pretty rough, especially after I left church school. I knew my mother loved me, but because she was out doing the very things that a loving, caring mother needed to do—earning enough money to provide for her children—

Chapter Seven

I didn't always feel loved. I felt like my father had abandoned me even before I was born, and though I never doubted that Mother loved me, the main things I could remember were the times I'd gotten in trouble and she had disciplined me.

Much of my rebellious attitude no doubt stemmed from the fact that Stan and I were alone a lot and missed having a "normal" family life. I felt like I was always looking for the end of the rainbow around the next bend, but never finding it. There was a loneliness deep down inside that went with me everywhere—even in the midst of a crowd. Sure I had a lot of good times going to movies and parties, but none of it ever left me feeling really satisfied with my life.

But when I met Jesus—and fell in love with Him—all that changed. The two months I had spent living as a totally committed Christian had been the sweetest, happiest days of my life. I had found a purpose for living and a Friend who went with me everywhere, filling the vacuum I had felt before. A plan had begun to formulate in my mind. I had always hoped to go to college, and now I planned to go to a Christian college where I hoped to meet and marry a man who was planning to be a minister—or maybe an evangelist. Surely God could use my musical talent if I were married to such a man. I could sing and help him win souls for the kingdom of God.

And I had thought that somehow, this opportunity to sing to others about the love of God that had made such a difference for me, would only add to the joy and contentment I had been feeling. Maybe it would even help open opportunities for me to serve God in new ways.

But the opposite happened.

I went away from that meeting feeling as dejected and discontented as I could ever remember. Somehow the peace and contentment I had been experiencing had evaporated, and I felt tears coming on. *What in the world could be wrong with me?* I wondered.

Then it was almost like the Holy Spirit spoke right to me. It wasn't that I heard a voice or anything, but I could sense God speaking to me, reminding me that Jesus and my ego couldn't sit on the throne together. I had let my head swell with all the fuss and praise.

I felt so dejected. Here I had thought I was serving the Lord, and yet I had let self creep in and steal center stage. *Did that mean I was an unfit vessel that would never be able to be used of God? Should I stop singing in public all together, just to be sure that I didn't end up on an ego trip?*

With these thoughts swirling in my head, I decided I needed some time alone with God. There was a large vineyard right next to the place where I was staying, and it seemed to offer the chance for some privacy and solitude, so I wandered down one of the rows, deep in thought. Midway down the row, the despair swept over me again, and I fell to my knees and just cried out to the Lord to help me.

I don't know how long I stayed there, kneeling on the soft earth, but it was long enough to get a few things sorted out with the Lord. I talked to Him as I would to a friend, telling Him my dilemma—I wanted to sing for Him, but I was afraid of what pride would do to me. I prayed, "Lord, if my voice is going to keep me out of heaven, take it from me!" And I believe God spoke back to me—not audibly—but in a way that I could hear and understand. "I'll take care of your ego," He said. "You leave that with Me."

When I left the vineyard, the feeling of peace and acceptance with God had returned, and I knew I could trust Him to take care of me whatever might come.

I've thanked the Lord many times in my years of ministry for that experience. I'm glad that it came to me so early in my career, because it taught me several important lessons. I not only learned to lean on Him to keep my pride from getting the best of me. I also learned that it's not safe to do what I call "slobbering" over people when they've done a good job up front. If I'm particularly blessed by a singer today, I'll go to them and tell them how much their song blessed me, and that I appreciate what they're doing, but I'm always careful not to be a stumbling block by helping to inflate someone's ego. The glory needs to go to the Lord who gave the gift.

Something else came out of that experience as well. It wasn't long before the phone started ringing at Mom's house, with people who had heard me sing at Lodi, or who had heard about my singing there, asking to talk to Del about moving her ministry to a whole new level. In the few short months since I had met Bob Thompson, my life had changed drastically. And it was about to change even more—if I'd let it.

Chapter Eight

The first time a man called from The Voice of Prophecy asking me to consider singing on the radio for that ministry, I wasn't even sure exactly what he was talking about. Sure, I had heard of H. M. S. Richards and the King's Heralds male gospel quartet, and I knew that theirs was one of the most popular Christian broadcasts on radio. Their program had been heard nationwide on the Mutual Broadcasting System since about the beginning of World War II and they were getting to be well known all around the world. But I hadn't really paid attention to what was going on with their program. I was mainly interested in The Quiet Hour and was perfectly content to continue working at the Pacific Greyhound office and singing on Pastor Tucker's broadcast until I could save up enough money to go to college. So, when the call came, I said that I had my plans laid out already, and I wasn't interested in moving to Los Angeles.

I thought that was the end of that, but a few days later the phone rang again and someone else—who must not have heard about my first response—was talking to me about possibly joining the staff of The Voice of Prophecy as a secretary and maybe once in a while singing for the broadcast. I politely explained that I'd already been approached about the possibility, and that I didn't think that was what the Lord had planned for my life, but I was honored that they would think of me.

There was more behind my hesitation than just not wanting to change the plans I had for my future. I knew that The Voice of Prophecy had one of the best music departments of any radio broadcast—religious or secular. The quartet was widely recognized as one of the finest on the air. I was full of self-doubt. I had never had a lick of musical training beyond a couple of violin lessons when I was eight years old. Mom had always wanted me to play the violin because it was her favorite instrument, but even at that early age I had some pretty strong opinions about music. And I knew I didn't want to play the violin. It looked too hard for me. I still remember the day she dragged me into a music store and parted with some hard-earned savings to get a little second-hand violin for me. When we left the store, I was screaming at the top of my lungs, "But I don't want to play the violin!"

You can lead a child to a violin, but you can't make her play. I suppose Mom was just too busy and too tired to enforce her decision that I was going to take lessons and practice the violin, because I can remember only a few lessons, and then the instrument disappeared and nothing more was said about it.

Now I regretted my stubbornness—not that I wished I knew how to play the violin—but if I'd just been more responsive, I could have at least had some training in how to read music. There was simply no way I could feel comfortable going to work with a group of professional musicians when all I knew how to do was memorize songs I'd heard someone else sing. Maybe if I could go to college first and take some music classes, then I'd feel more comfortable.

The third time someone called from The Voice of Prophecy, I began to wonder whether any of the people down there talked to each other. Didn't they know that I had already turned down two invitations to come and join them? The caller assured me that he had heard about my two previous responses. Somehow there was still a very strong impression at the ministry—an impression they felt the Lord had given to them—that I was the person with the right female voice they needed to round out their music department. Now I was in a dilemma. If the leaders down at The Voice of Prophecy were that strongly impressed that I ought to join them, who was I—a brand-new baby Christian— to say that they were wrong and I was right? But still, my mind was pretty well made up. I planned to begin college that very September, and the college I had chosen was north of Oakland. Los Angeles was south. I knew what direction I planned to go. I politely turned down my caller and said that maybe, after I had finished college, I might reconsider.

But he wouldn't be put off that easily. He asked me to pray about it for a couple of days and promised to call back and see whether the Lord had been able to change my mind.

I hung up the phone and flopped down on the couch in our living room, then got up and paced the floor a couple times and headed for the door, intending to go out for a walk.

"Something's troubling you, isn't it, Del?" Mom asked. In fact, she had noticed a marked change coming over me ever since the first time I'd had a call from The Voice of Prophecy. There had even been times when she had seen me pacing the floor, wringing my hands, and crying. And I don't cry easily. I can be heartbroken and I don't usually cry. So she knew something was really bothering me deeply.

When I didn't respond, she said, "Was that the people from The Voice of Prophecy again?"

"Yes," I said. "But you know I plan to go to college this fall. I just don't see how the Lord could be calling me to move down there and join their ministry."

"Then why are you so troubled?" she asked.

"I don't know . . . it's just that . . . well, how am I supposed to know what's right?"

"You know what you remind me of?"

"What?"

"You remind me of Jonah running away from Nineveh," she said. "Is there any chance you're running away from the Lord, Del?"

"I don't know. I don't think so."

"Well, you pray about it, and I'm sure the Lord will reveal the right thing to you," Mom said.

I had a long walk that evening, thinking and praying. And I didn't sleep very well for the next couple of nights.

Then the phone rang again, and it was the friendly voice from The Voice of Prophecy. "Have you reconsidered, Del? Is there any chance we can get you to move down here and join our ministry?"

"Um, well, I've, uh, I've prayed a lot about it," I said. "And I guess, maybe. Well, maybe yes, that is the way the Lord is leading in my life."

"Great! How soon do you think you could be here? How about the middle of next month? The Chief—that's Pastor Richards—will be back home from Europe by then, and I know he'll want to meet you and hear you sing."

"That should be fine," I said.

When I hung up the phone, I couldn't possibly imagine just how big a change my life had just taken, or where it would lead me. I didn't feel an immediate sense of assurance that I had done the right thing. The middle of September was supposed to find me headed north to college. Now it would find me headed the opposite direction. I had lived in Oakland for almost my whole life. All my friends were there. I had seldom traveled outside the Bay Area, except for a trip back to Java, South Dakota, my mother's hometown, when I was twelve. What would it be like to move five hundred miles south and live in Los Angeles, make all new friends, and start work full time in a Christian ministry?

And how would I tell my friends here that I would be moving away? What would they think of me at The Quiet Hour—would they think I was a traitor for joining up with another radio ministry? Sure, we were all on God's team, working for the same cause, but I had spent enough time dating marines and sailors to know that there's a strong rivalry between the various branches of our nation's military. What would Pastor Tucker—my friend, confidant, and mentor—think?

When I broke the news to him, he looked disappointed and happy all at the same time.

"I'm happy for you—but sad for me," he said. "You know we would have loved to take you on full time here, if only we could afford it.

But I don't see any way that we could promise you full-time work here. This must be the Lord's leading. I know He has a place for you and your talent in His work, and though I wish it could be here, well, maybe this is for the best. I want you to know I'll support you in your decision, Del."

Those were not idle words. When it was time for me to move, Pastor Tucker loaded up all my worldly goods in his personal car and drove me to Los Angeles himself! I learned years later that Pastor T. had gotten much of his inspiration—and a good deal of advice— from H. M. S. Richards of The Voice of Prophecy when he was starting The Quiet Hour. So there was no kind of rivalry between the two ministries. Pastors Tucker and Richards were only too glad to help each other out whenever they had a chance.

Chapter Nine

Y ou might think that, judging by all the effort people at The Voice of Prophecy put into persuading me to come and join their ministry, everyone down there must have thought that I was just the cat's meow—just exactly what the ministry needed—and that the first thing they'd do on my arrival would be to give me a tour of the recording studio and put me to work producing records.

Well, that's not quite what happened. In fact, there wasn't much of a studio at The Voice of Prophecy (I'll call the ministry the VOP from here on out to save ink!) at that time. Recording technology was still pretty much in its infancy. In fact, tape recording machines were not available in the U. S. yet. Every radio program you heard in those days was either a live broadcast or a long-playing disk recording.

Because the VOP was on all across the country, the entire program had to be produced twice each Sunday morning, once at 6:30 for the Central and Eastern time zones, then again at 8:30 for the Mountain and Pacific zones.

And we couldn't broadcast directly from our own studio. Those who were going to be on the program on a given Sunday would have to get up very early, meet at the VOP headquarters, and then carpool down to Hollywood to a broadcasting studio. From there the program was networked, live, to affiliate stations all across the country. Most stations had no recording facilities at all. Whenever we wanted to have an archival copy of one of our broadcasts, we'd have to make arrangements with a company in Hollywood that specialized in doing air checks—that is, they would record the program onto a huge sixteen-inch acetate disk that looked like an oversize LP album. They would record the program off the air as it was being broadcast. Each of those large disks could hold just one thirty-minute program on each side.

Leston Post, a recording engineer for Chapel Records, had built an experimental tape recorder. Bob Seamount, second tenor of the King's Heralds, was uniquely gifted in many things including electronics. He built another experimental recorder for us to use in rehearsals as we prepared our programs.

We could also use an acetate disk recorder to prerecord programs, but the quality wasn't as good as a live broadcast, so we didn't do that often. Even when traveling, the team would try to make arrangements to go into a radio studio wherever they were and produce a live broadcast.

It wasn't until 1949 that tape recorders started to become available commercially, and that was only because Bing Crosby went to Europe and saw a German-made Ampex recorder. He came back to Hollywood and announced that he wasn't going to continue to do his program unless it could be prerecorded. Pastor Richards always liked to be on the cutting edge of things—that's why he began radio broadcasting clear back in 1929, when most Christians still thought of radio as a tool of the devil that we ought to stay as far away from as we could. When he heard that Bing Crosby's program was being prerecorded, it wasn't long until some folks from the VOP went down to Hollywood to have a look at the equipment. At that time the new VOP building was under construction in Glendale, California, and it was resolved that the studios there would have Ampex recorders—even though installing them would cost about ten thousand dollars—to make it possible to prerecord programs. But up until 1950, when we moved into those new studios, almost everything had to be done live. Even after that, the program was still produced live twice every Sunday morning for several more years, but we could use some recorded music or prepare a tape for times when we would be out of town.

The King's Heralds, accompanied by Al Avila on the organ, were known worldwide for their beautiful music. You can read quite a bit about their history in Bob Edwards's book about the life of H. M. S. Richards, titled simply *H. M. S. Richards*. Bob himself had joined the quartet just a few months before I arrived on the scene in September of 1947.

Suffice it to say that things had been pretty turbulent for the VOP, and especially for the music department, in the years just prior to 1947. The Lone Star Four, who became the King's Heralds in 1937, sang on the broadcast until 1939, and then members had dropped out and been replaced one by one. Then in the middle '40s, a well-meaning committee of administrators back on the East Coast decided that they knew more about how to create beautiful music than the musicians and started rearranging the quartet to their liking. I've heard it said that a camel is a horse designed by a committee—no offense to camels intended—but it seems like a good analogy. The committee members didn't seem to understand that a quartet has to come together of its own accord and learn to work together and harmonize. You can't just pick a bass, a baritone, and two tenors, and tell them to work it out. There's a lot more to getting a pleasing sound than that, and that finally became apparent.

It was about 1947 when someone decided the broadcast would use a variety of musicians, possibly a choral group, instead of just four members of the quartet, and that could have had something to do with my being brought on board. But things were in too much of a turmoil for me to be welcomed with open arms. I think all the members of the music department felt kind of insecure at that time, never knowing when or whether they'd be called on to sing on the broadcast again. It wasn't until the middle of 1949—nearly two years after my arrival—that things finally settled down when Wayne Hooper, who had been in the quartet from 1944 to the middle of 1947, was invited to come back to the VOP and form a new quartet. Wayne is a baritone, and he selected Bob Edwards for his first tenor,

Bob Seamount for second tenor, and Jerry Dill for the bass. That King's Heralds group stayed together for the next twelve years, and they're probably the ones that many old fans of the VOP remember as *The* King's Heralds.

Even after Wayne arrived and formed the new quartet, it wasn't easy for me to work into the program on a regular basis. It took a while for things to settle down in the music department, and I think Wayne was really focused on getting his group working together well. It wasn't that anyone treated me unkindly or anything like that. I've said over and over again through the years—they were all nice to me in an impersonal way. Remember, throughout its history up to that point, music on *The Voice of Prophecy* had been almost exclusively male vocals.

The official call to the VOP had been an invitation to come and be a secretary there—with the understanding that they'd use my musical talents as well. At least that's what I thought. But I ended up singing on the broadcast only a few times in 1948 and 1949. My main duties were all secretarial.

One of my early bosses at first was Pastor H. M. J. Richards, the father of the VOP's founder, H. M. S. Richards. The senior Pastor Richards was well up in years by then, but he still had an active part in the broadcast each week, usually offering the prayer. He was well respected by everyone at the VOP, but I guess you could say it hadn't been particularly easy for him to get a secretary who was fully to his liking. And on the other hand, quite a few of the women who had been assigned to him had asked to be reassigned after only a short time. I suppose you could say he was a little on the crotchety side by that time.

He liked to dictate long, flowery letters, and at first I dutifully took them down in shorthand and typed them word for word. But then I began to wonder about what kind of impression his letters were making on their recipients. I didn't want my boss to be viewed as a repetitious old man who was starting to lose it, so one day I took the liberty of shortening one of his letters and reorganizing it so it flowed a bit better. I put it on his desk for his signature, and just a few minutes later he marched up to my desk, pointed his finger at me, and said, "Young lady, you are not to change my letters. You say exactly what I say!"

I don't doubt that a number of other secretaries might have tried the same thing with him with the same sort of results. Perhaps after his stern lecture they had just gone to the bathroom and had a good cry and come back and done as they were told—at least until they could find another job. But I'd had quite a few years' experience writing letters for my boss at Pacific Greyhound, and besides that, I've got 100 percent German blood running in my veins, and I wasn't about to be pushed around quite so easily. I looked up at him and said, as sweetly as I could, "Pastor Richards, it seems to me that that letter was too repetitive. If you want me to say just exactly what you say, I'll do it, but a good secretary tries to make her boss look good, and I want to make you look good. If you don't want me to make you look good, I'll do it your way."

It seemed to catch him totally by surprise, and he didn't have a response, except to say "Hmph," and turn around and go back to his office. I continued to edit his letters after that, and he never complained again. In fact, we became good friends. I remember one time when I took some vacation time and went up to visit my mom and friends in Oakland, I got a letter from him. He started it out, "Dear Slave!" We would joke around and kid like that for the rest of his life.

But my life at the VOP that first year wasn't all drudgery and dictation. There were a few single fellows on the staff, and one of them in particular seemed to take a special interest in me. I've thought long and hard about this, and decided I wouldn't share his real name, even though he is no longer living, because I wouldn't want to hurt any of his family members, so I'll just call him Tom.

Tom was about my age, and a very charming young fellow, who enjoyed music as much as I did. We sang duets together, and everyone said we sounded just great. It wasn't long before an office romance began to bloom, and we'd see each other outside of office hours as well. He'd call me up every morning and declare his undying love for me. I began to think that this was the way the Lord was leading in my life. I had wanted to go to college and meet and marry a minister, but maybe this was God's better plan. Here was a young man already involved in ministry. It seemed like we just might be a match made in heaven. And from the things he said to me, I began to get the impression that he felt the same way about it.

It's hard for me to tell this part of the story even this many years later. Just when it seemed like things were going to get really serious between us—we'd even discussed marriage a time or two—all of a sudden he dropped me like a hot potato. It seemed like I held about as much interest to him as an old, dirty shirt. He wouldn't come to my office and say Hi anymore. Wouldn't invite me to go places in the evening. If he'd see me coming down the hall toward him at work, he'd duck into someone else's office so he wouldn't have to make eye contact. There was no explanation. No goodbye, nothing. He just started ignoring me.

I tried to confront him and find out what had happened, but to no avail.

Believe me, that hurt.

Around the office I put on a brave face, like nothing was wrong. But at night I often cried myself to sleep. I just could not understand what had gone wrong, and I couldn't get over it easily. Remember, I'd always felt like I'd been rejected by my own father, and Mom was gone so much. It was hard for me to deal with being rejected again— for no apparent reason.

It wasn't until a year or two later that I found out what had gone wrong. Tom confided in a mutual friend, and that friend came to me and explained—just out of kindness to me—because she knew how badly I had been hurt.

It seems that when I first came to the VOP, I was regarded as a secretary, not a singer, and that suited Tom fine. But as soon as I started getting invitations to sing at churches and large gatherings in the area and became well known, he became uncomfortable. Tom confessed to his friend, "I just want to marry a nobody."

Finding out what had gone wrong helped me a little bit—at least I didn't feel quite so much like I was some sort of reject that no one could ever truly love. But why couldn't he have explained his feelings to me? Why did he just leave me hanging like that? Oh well, I got over it with time.

It probably wasn't long after the time with Tom that I began to question whether the Lord had really been in the call to the VOP. I had dedicated my life, and my musical talent, to serving Him, but it just didn't seem that this was the place those talents were going to be used. I figured I could be a secretary anywhere, so why should I stay in Los Angeles, so far from my friends and family? When Pastor Tucker drove me down there, he made sure I understood that if I ever decided to return to the Oakland area, he'd be more than delighted to use me on The Quiet Hour broadcast again.

So, after giving it the good old college try at the VOP for a year or so, I decided I didn't belong there and began making plans for a move back to Oakland.

Chapter Ten

The associate speaker for The Voice of Prophecy in those days was Pastor Elmer Walde. He served as the announcer on the radio broadcast and would sometimes preach the sermon as well when H. M. S. Richards was out of town. He was a kind, gentle man whom everyone loved. In fact, he was almost as much loved and respected as The Chief—H. M. S. Richards—himself. And boy could he preach! If the two men traveled to the same place for speaking appointments, many people considered it a toss-up as to whom to go and hear. They certainly were both worth hearing!

Elmer seemed to take a special interest in me right from the start and often invited me to go with him and provide music when he took speaking appointments in the area. He was a man I knew I could confide in, so when I began to get discouraged with my prospects in the music department, I went to see him.

Whenever I'd go into his office, he'd always have me sit down to talk to him—he just had a way of helping people feel relaxed and comfortable around him. But my decision to leave the VOP and go back to Oakland hadn't come easily. I had prayed a lot about it and had spent quite a little time pacing the floor thinking about it. So I wasn't in a particularly calm mood when I finally got up my courage to go talk to him.

I knocked on his office door, and when he invited me in, I marched right in and stood in front of his desk. "Elmer," I said, "I want you to know I've made a decision, and I want you to be the first to know about it."

He looked up at me, no doubt sensing the tension in my voice, and stood up—but not in a confrontational way. He just stood up calmly and motioned with his hand. "Sit down, Del," he said. "And tell me all about it."

I didn't want to sit down. I wanted to make my announcement quickly and walk out. I wouldn't slam the door behind me or anything like that. I wasn't angry. I just wanted to get it over with and not have to persuade anyone that I was making the right decision.

But I couldn't refuse the chair he offered. When I'd taken my seat, Elmer sat down too. "Now, tell me what's on your mind," he said.

"Well, I think you know, Elmer, that when I came here, it was with the understanding that I would be able to use my singing talent for the Lord. I was led to believe that I would be singing on the broadcast. But they've used me only a couple of times in the past year. Frankly, I don't think the people in the music department much care for me. And I don't need this. Pastor Tucker promised me that if I ever came back to Oakland, he'd find a place for me on their broadcast, and I feel like maybe that's the way the Lord is leading me right now. So, I just came to tell you that I'm going to be leaving soon. I wanted you to be the first to know."

With that I started to stand up to leave, but he motioned with his hand for me to stay, then got up and partially closed his office door so that people in the hall couldn't overhear what we were talking about.

"Del," he said. "I fully understand what's bothering you. I've noticed that they haven't been using you on the broadcast. But I've sure appreciated having you come with me and sing when I take speaking appointments. It's been enjoyable working together, hasn't it?"

I had to admit that I had really enjoyed working with him.

"I'll tell you what," he continued. "I really believe in you, Del. And I think the broadcast needs you. But it's going to take a little time to work these things out. There's probably going to be some changes made in the music department pretty soon, and I think things will work out if you'll give it a little more time. In fact, I'll go to work on it myself and keep reminding them to include you on the program from time to time. How would that be?"

"I don't want anyone to have to sell me," I responded. "If they don't see any use for me, and if I don't seem like someone they can use, I don't want someone else pushing me in."

"But what if it's God's will, Del? I really believe that God has a place for you here. Won't you stay a little longer and see what develops?"

I just couldn't turn him down, so I reluctantly agreed and put my plans for a move on hold—at least for the time being.

It wasn't long after that that I was transferred from being H. M. J. Richards's secretary to working for a human dynamo by the name of Bessie Flaiz-Detamore. She was the stepmother of the well-known VOP evangelist Fordyce Detamore, and she had more energy than just about anyone I've ever met. She was the head of the VOP's correspondence Bible school, which had been started in 1942. It's usually said that Fordyce was the one who started the school, but I've always thought that perhaps Bessie had a lot to do with planting the seed of the idea. One thing's for sure, she had a lot to do with seeing to it that the school ran well. She was always coming up with some great new idea, and she could keep me busy, plus four or five other girls.

The opportunity to work for Mrs. Detamore turned out to be a real blessing for me, because I got to take down her dictation and type up her letters for her. I learned so much from her, because she took the time to answer a lot of letters from people who were taking the Bible lessons and had written in for special counsel on some question or personal problem. Bessie knew just what to say and how to say it, and it wasn't long before I had memorized whole paragraphs from her letters. They would stand me in good stead for the rest of my life as I encountered and tried to help people with similar needs.

When I first arrived at the VOP, someone in the business office had made arrangements for me to be able to rent a room in a large house that was owned by the organization. Fortunately, it was quite close to the office in Glendale, so I could walk back and forth to work. Two other women employees also rented rooms there, and that's how I got acquainted with Doris Crawford. She was a bit older than I, but the two of us really hit it off and became good friends.

Not too long after I moved into the house, word came down from the business office that the house was going to be rented out to a minister and his family who were coming to join the staff, so we gals needed to find apartments to rent on our own. Because Doris and I got along so well together, we decided to pool our funds and get an apartment together, and it was through Doris that I met some of the most important people in my life.

We'd been sharing the apartment for probably a year or a bit longer, when Doris came to me one day with a very concerned look on her face. She proceeded to tell me about her sister-in-law, Bernice Davidson. Bernice was married to Doris's brother Keith, but things weren't going well in the family. Doris's brother was quite violent and abusive toward Bernice and her three daughters, and Bernice had come to the point where she knew she just had to move out. "She hasn't anywhere to go and not a penny to her name," Doris said. "What do you think, Del? Do you think it would be all right if she moved in with us—just until she can get a job and get back on her feet?"

How could I say No to a request like that? The only reason my own mother had been able to survive and raise Stanley and me was that family members and others had been willing to help her out when she had to leave my father.

So that's how I got my ready-made family. I believe it was in 1949 that twelve-year-old Ann, nine-year-old Carol, and four-year-old Beth and their mother moved into the little apartment Doris and I had been sharing.

It made for pretty cramped quarters for a bit, but we didn't figure it would last long. Bernice was a bright, hardworking woman, and we knew that she would soon be able to be out on her own again.

But that's not the way it worked out. In fact, Doris was the one who moved out first. She had decided that she wanted to be a nurse, so she moved up to St. Helena, California, and enrolled in nursing classes at the sanitarium there. Bernice and I became lifelong friends, and her daughters became like my own daughters—or at least nieces. They are very precious to me to this day.

We shared that little apartment for several months after Doris moved out, then found a roomier place. Meanwhile, I was able to find work for Bernice at the VOP in the correspondence Bible school, and when Bessie retired a few years later, guess who took over as the head of the school—my friend Bernice. She really was a brilliant woman and a hard worker who just needed the right opportunities to allow her talents to blossom. But life never was very easy for her, as a single mother with three girls to bring up. She wanted to do right by them, so she took on extra jobs in order to make it possible to send the girls to church school. For several years she would leave the VOP after a long day of work supervising the Bible school and go directly to the nearby sanitarium, where she would work for several more hours, help-ing put the patients to bed for the night.

With Bernice working so hard, I got to play mom to the girls quite a bit. Sometimes they would even go with me on weekend trips, but they were never a bit of trouble. I can still remember seeing them sitting like perfect angels in the pew while I was up front singing. They seemed to understand that their mother was having a hard time making ends meet, and they wanted to do whatever they could to help out. One day Bernice and I came home and found that there were no pictures hanging on our walls anymore. It was a great mystery until we asked the girls about it. They announced that they had done us the great favor of taking the pictures down the street, selling them to neighbors in order to help out with household expenses!

Oh, how we laughed over that one! We had to assure the girls that we really appreciated their attempt to help out, but would they please go back down the street and see whether they could possibly buy the pictures back? Things might be a bit tight right now, but we'd manage somehow, and if we needed to start selling household items, we'd be sure to let them know, since they seemed to have a real talent for it.

It was about this time that we introduced another member into our family. Bernice and I had discussed it and decided it would be a good idea for the girls to have a pet, and some friends mentioned that they had several cats to give away, so we went to have a look. I immediately fell in love with a little long-haired calico, but the people weren't sure they wanted to part with that particular one because it was unusually beautiful. I remember saying to Bernice, "Either we take that one, or none at all."

So we went home empty-handed. A couple of weeks later though, the friends changed their minds and said we could have the little calico. Not long before that Bernice had had some correspondence with a Bible student named Boleslaw Fries, and we thought that was such an unusual name that I always remembered it, and decided to name the cat after him. Boleslaw was a beautiful girl kitty who had several litters. But none of her children were as pretty as she was. As I think back on it, she didn't deserve such a dumb name as Boleslaw, which didn't even sound like a girl cat! But she didn't seem to mind. We just called her "Bole."

I've had several cats through the years, but never one so smart as Boleslaw. Carol, Bernice's middle daughter, saw how smart that cat was, and started teaching her tricks. Some people don't believe me when I tell them that that cat could roll over, jump through a hoop, and even play the piano on command, but she could. I would tell her to play the piano, and she'd get up on the piano bench and put one paw on the keys and make a little plink, then look at me and meow and hold her mouth open, waiting for a treat. But I'd say, "That's not good enough, Bole." Then she'd growl at me, and put both paws on the keys, and play a little bit more to earn her reward. A number of friends came to our home to see this performance and said they had never seen anything like it. She really won a place in all of our hearts, and when she finally got old and sick and died, I was just plain brokenhearted over the loss. I'll never forget what Brad Braley, the organist who accompanied me for many years, said when he saw how sad I looked. He said, "Del, I believe you'll have another cat just like Boleslaw in heaven."

"But I don't want another cat just like Boleslaw," I said. "I want Boleslaw to be there!"

So Brad said he thought that maybe the Lord would make special arrangements for me so I could have my little kitty for all eternity. I don't know if that's true or not, but it made me feel better at the time.

Chapter Eleven

Having Bernice and the girls move in with me gave me a bit more of a reason to stay at the VOP instead of heading back to Oakland, but I still wasn't completely satisfied that my talents were being used in the way that the Lord would have them be. I probably went back to Pastor Walde's office three or four more times, each time intent on turning in my resignation, but he'd always get me to sit down and talk for a bit, until he could find some way to settle me down. He said he just knew that God wanted me there, and that He hadn't made a mistake when He led me to accept the call.

And it turned out that he was right after all.

There finally came a day, probably about three years after I had arrived at the VOP, when Wayne Hooper, who was in charge of planning the music for the program and doing the arrangements for the quartet, came into my office and sat down. "I want to talk to you, Del," he said.

"Yes," I said, giving him my attention but not sounding too enthusiastic, I suppose. It wasn't that I had anything against him, but I did feel very frustrated. I was pouring my whole life into my ministry at the VOP, but it didn't seem like anyone except Pastor Walde really appreciated it. I would work a full eight-hour day Monday through Friday. Then on the weekends I'd be expected to travel and sing somewhere, often getting back home late on Sunday, only to have to start the week all over again at my desk, bright and cheery by eight o'clock Monday morning. And I have to tell you, I'm really not a morning person. Years later, when I was recording regularly with the quartet, Jim McClintock was the bass. It was well known that neither Jim nor I were morning people. But one day he showed up at the studio with a song he'd written. When the other quartet members asked what the title was, he said, "Morning Moments With Jesus." Suddenly the whole studio erupted in laughter. I think we were almost rolling on the floor before it was over—it just struck us as so funny. The quartet almost always did their recording in the morning, so we all were well aware of Jim's struggle to be awake so early.

I must tell you though, that this is a wonderful song. Jim has written several songs that I have recorded and used for many years. We can't help it that we're not morning people.

I don't remember if it was morning or afternoon when Wayne came into my office that day, but I do know that what he said caught me totally by surprise. "Del," he said, "we need to talk." Knowing he had not been eager to include anyone but the quartet in the music department, I wondered what we needed to talk about.

"I owe you an apology," he continued.

That got my attention, but I just looked at him quizzically.

"When I first met you," he said, "I was just trying to get the new quartet all set up, and I have to admit, I just didn't see any light in the idea of adding a woman's voice to the broadcast. It was nothing against you—understand. It was just that I was interested in working only with the quartet, and I felt like bringing you here was someone else's idea, and I just didn't want to deal with it at the time." He paused and looked down at the floor for a moment before continuing.

"But I was wrong," he said. "I've been watching you, and I've come to realize that I was wrong. I really believe that the Lord called you here and that He has a place for you in the music ministry of The Voice of Prophecy. I want you to know that you can count on me. If there's anything I can do to help you further your career as a singer, I'll do it."

Chapter Eleven

And Wayne, bless his heart, was true to his word. Right away he started including me on the broadcast almost every week in solos, duets, and five-part songs with the King's Heralds. That meant I started spending more and more of my time down in the recording studio. And it also meant that Wayne became my first real music teacher. Boy was he hard on me! And rightly so. I didn't know a thing about music. I had always been able to rely on my ability to learn a song and harmony by listening. He had a hard job ahead of him, trying to make a singer out of me. There were some recording sessions where I almost ended up in tears—but I wouldn't cry in front of him—I saved the tears for later when I was alone. He wasn't mean, but he was very particular.

There were times when I wished I could take a year off from recording and just have Wayne coach me outside of studio hours. Then I could come back and do it right without having to be corrected mid-song all the time, but there was no time for that. We had to produce a new program every week, so that meant that all the teaching had to be on-the-job training. And in addition to producing the Sunday broadcast each week, we also recorded the music for the Spanish-language broadcast that was aired in South and Central America. Every Tuesday was devoted to recording songs in Spanish or other languages with the help of a tutor who made sure we pronounced the words exactly right. Imagine the stress of trying to learn to sing up to Wayne's high musical standards and at the same time having to please a perfectionist language tutor!

It was hard at the time, but I realize now that I have a lot to thank Wayne for. When I go back and listen to some of the earliest recordings I made, I recognize how much I needed to learn. And frankly, I guess I can't blame Wayne for being hesitant to use me. He's a real professional, and he knows just how to coax the sound he wants out of other musicians. Through the years Wayne and his wife, Harriet, and I came to be close friends. I have often been a part of their family gatherings. When Wayne dropped out of the quartet at the end of 1962 in order to be able to devote more time to directing the music department, I became his secretary and continued in that position until his retirement. Wayne became well known in Christian music circles for his arrangements of music for quartets and larger groups. He also composed the song "We Have This Hope" that has become a mainstay at Seventh-day Adventist gatherings all over the world. He celebrated his eighty-second birthday not long ago, and he continues to be active in the music field. One big project he completed recently was transferring all of the songs from the VOP music library from tape to digital media, producing more than 160 CDs of music (3,600 songs) recorded by VOP musicians between 1950 and 1982.

When the VOP moved into their newly constructed headquarters building in Glendale, California, July 1, 1950, there was great rejoicing in the music department. Finally we had a real studio all our own, with a genuine Ampex tape recorder that we could use to record songs.

Before the advent of tape machines, any programs that were pre-recorded to be played while some of our radio group were out of town had to be recorded on the sixteen-inch acetate disks I described earlier. That meant we had to go down to Hollywood to the Radio Recorders Studio and record the program straight through with no interruptions. Many times we would get almost all the way through when someone would miss a cue, or something would go wrong in one of the songs. That meant the disk had to be thrown away, and we had to start over again at the beginning and do the whole program again. With the Ampex tape machines, we could stop and start, cut and splice, and produce programs right in our own studios, saving ourselves hours and hours of repetitious work.

The same was true of any music we wanted to use. Before we had the tape machines, we did almost all the music live as part of the broadcast. But that meant many hours of practice beforehand to make sure we always had a professional sound. Now, with the new recording equipment, we could begin to think of building up a library of songs that we could use over and over again, without having to perform them live each time. And it wasn't long before someone got the idea of creating record albums and selling them to the public. The King's Heralds released their first long-playing album, *Oh Little Town of Bethlehem* just in time for Christmas in

1950. They went on to release two more quartet albums. Then, in May 1951, The Voice of Prophecy newsletter included the following announcement:

Another Voice of Prophecy Record Album

The latest album by the King's Heralds quartet and Del Delker, contralto, brings you real variety in choice arrangements of familiar hymns. This album (No. 102) consists of two five-part numbers, "When the Shadows Flee Away," and "My Home Sweet Home"; a duet, "The Hands of the Saviour," by Del Delker and Bob Seamount, second tenor in the quartet; and three quartet numbers, "Hold the Fort," "Master, the Tempest Is Raging," and "Follow On."

These six phonograph recordings are on ten-inch disks, made of flexible, non-breakable material. You can obtain this attractive album for $3.50, postage prepaid. If you live in California, add 12 cents for sales tax. When ordering, please request the album by its number and be sure to send your order to The Voice of Prophecy Recording Company, Box 1511, Glendale, California.

The album was actually number 103. Someone on the editorial staff must not have checked their facts with the music department, but that's OK. What the announcement meant to me was that finally I was being recognized and accepted as one of the official musicians of The Voice of Prophecy radio broadcast. Elmer Walde had been right. If I would just be patient, God would have a way of working things out for the best.

I've had to learn that lesson over and over in life. I tend to want to work things out on my own, on my schedule. Patience isn't a natural trait for me. But the Lord's still working on me.

There was another area of my life that I needed to be patient about as well—an area that I know a lot of people have been curious about.

Chapter Twelve

I've been very hesitant to tell about this part of my life, because it's very private, and I haven't wanted to share it with anyone except those who know me best and lived through these experiences with me. But some of my closest friends have insisted that I share just a bit of my romantic life, so people will know that I'm a normal human being. When I was a teenager and in my early twenties, I was a fun-loving party girl, I guess you could say. I liked to date a lot of different guys and didn't have much interest in settling down and starting a family.

When I gave my heart to the Lord, though, that began to change. I mentioned before that I thought it was God's plan for me to go away to a college, where I hoped to find a ministerial student to marry. I could picture myself serving as a pastor's wife, bringing up a family, and, of course, singing in church and at evangelistic meetings my husband would hold.

The call to move to the VOP, of course, interrupted those plans. But it didn't do away with my nesting instinct. Bernice and her little girls made a nice addition to my home, but that wasn't what I was really looking for. I still wanted to meet Mr. Right and raise a family of my own.

There were a couple of single fellows about my age on the VOP staff when I arrived there, but no serious prospects of marriage ever developed with them. I thought things were going that direction with the fellow I called Tom in chapter nine, but then he dropped me like a hot potato.

Through the years there have been many other opportunities for me to pursue romantic love as well, but for one reason or another, none of them has ever led to marriage. The life I've led, which has kept me in front of large crowds even up till this day, has been rich and fulfilling in many ways, but you've got to understand that having a high profile often interferes with one's private life.

To start with, being a public figure tends to attract a certain type of interest that's not always desirable. There have been countless suitors who have written to me, absolutely sure that the Lord had given them guidance that they ought to marry me. Some have written love poems to me. One of my favorites went like this: "Lift up your optimistic and lovable eyes, and peer into a new year of glorious uncertainties." In another letter the same man wrote, "The air I breathe in a room empty of you is unclean."

I'm not sure exactly what he intended, or whether he thought it was my responsibility to act as an air filter for him, but I didn't feel much of an urge to jump on my white stallion and ride to his rescue.

It must have been when I was about forty that I was traveling on a long itinerary one time. Bernice always opened my mail while I was gone, because often it included contributions that needed to be turned in. One day she found two letters in the same batch of mail. Both of them came from men who were absolutely certain that the Lord had spoken to them and told them that they were to marry me.

Bernice always was a quick-witted person, and suddenly she had her own inspiration of how to handle that particular situation. She simply took the letter from Man A, put it in an envelope and addressed it to Man B. And then she took Man B's letter and sent it to Man A. No comment, nothing. Just put both of them in the mail and let them do their work. Needless to say, I never heard from either A or B again.

I wish it had been so easy with all of the would-be suitors. Here's a little secret that up till now only a few of my closest friends have known. In the book *Blue Highways*, well-known author William Least

Heat Moon tells about a long trip he took all around the United States. The book tells about many interesting people he met along the way. One of the characters he spends a couple of chapters on is a Seventh-day Adventist hitchhiker that he picked up near Moscow, Idaho. In the course of their conversation, William's guest tried repeatedly to sign him up for free Bible lessons from The Voice of Prophecy. When William asked where he was headed for, the man said he was on his way to El Salvador in Central America (even though he was headed north at the moment) to marry his fiancée. " 'My fiancée lives in San Salvador,' the hitchhiker explained. 'I'm going there to get married and bring Carmen back if I can raise the money. She's a wonderful woman. Her love freed me from a ten-year obsession with a gospel singer' " (p. 158).

Boy do I wish!

I mean I wish it were true that Carmen's love had freed that man of his obsession. Because I'm the gospel singer he was obsessed with. That book was published in 1982, so I know that William Least Heat Moon met the hitchhiker more than twenty years ago, and the man still writes letters to me, declaring his love for me. I understand that he married Carmen, but that they separated a few years later. I don't read his letters anymore; they are very crude and raunchy. I only wrote to him once. I said, "Mr. ____, a gentleman never forces his attentions on a lady." He wrote back and said, "Woman, if I weren't a gentleman, I'd come and kick the ____ out of you!"

All I can say is I hope and pray that someday he will find true deliverance from his obsession.

There was another man at a certain camp meeting. I could always count on him. He'd be sitting on the front row, and as soon as I'd stand up to sing, he'd go into an epileptic fit. Fortunately, I don't affect any other men that way. But there was another camp meeting where they had to give me a twenty-four-hour guard because of a fellow who thought he was in love with me.

While there have been many men who have been attracted by the thought of dating or marrying me simply because they thought of me as a high-profile person, others have had a problem with whatever level of fame they perceived me to have. Tom wasn't the only one who eventually backed away because I was well known. A close friend once confided in me that one of my potential suitors had said to him, "Nobody wants to be Mr. Del Delker, you know."

Many people seem to think that being what they call a "high-profile person" must be wonderful—all the fame and adoring crowds and accolades must be a dream come true. And I have to say that my life "up front" has had many rewards. But notoriety has its drawbacks too. I can't say that I wish I had been able to fulfill my original dream of just settling down as a minister's wife and raising a family. I feel that the Lord chose me for the particular role He wanted me to play in life, and I'm content with that. Whenever Pastor Richards would speak to groups of ministerial students, he liked to tell them that they shouldn't go into the ministry unless it was the only thing they could do. What he meant was that one shouldn't choose to serve the Lord unless they know for sure that God had called them to that form of ministry, and they'd be miserable doing anything else.

Well, that was the case with me. I tried and tried to resist the Lord's call when it came at first. But I was miserable. Even after I began work at the VOP, I often considered leaving, but somehow I was always persuaded to stay on. And now, even though I officially retired a dozen years ago, after more than forty-two years of service, I still enjoy going out and singing for my Lord on a fairly regular basis.

But being the focus of so much attention can be stressful too. People expect you to be some sort of saint or something. I've traveled all over the world, and some places I've sensed that as soon as I stepped off the airplane, certain ones were looking me up and down to see whether I had too much makeup on, whether my skirt was too short, or perhaps too tight. It hurts when people put that kind of pressure on and want to judge you by your exterior. I recognize that as a public figure, representing my church, it's important to always look nice, and to try to avoid giving offense. But you never can keep all the people happy all the time.

I tried hard, at first, to live up to all those expectations. Somehow I got the idea in my head that if I was going to be a gospel singer, I had to look the part. And to me that meant conservative, conservative, conservative. The only thing I'd wear was white blouses and loose black skirts. I suppose it was kind of a reaction to the way I had lived before my conversion. Finally, a minister's wife, Martha Bietz, took me aside and asked, "Del, why do you always dress the same? You're just a young girl, and you ought to dress like one. Lighten up and look and act your age!"

I appreciated her counsel and went right out and bought a red dress! I think I also started to smile and laugh a little more.

But others haven't always been so kind and caring in trying to straighten me out.

In fact, one of the best and worst experiences of my entire ministry came as a result of some of the criticism that came my way. After I'd been at the VOP for several years, I started to get a series of poison pen letters, accusing me of various sins. One time I went to The Chief and told him about it and showed the letter to him. He said he'd already seen a copy of it and thrown it in the wastepaper basket. "I didn't even show it to Mabel," he said. That caught me by surprise, but what he said next has stuck with me. "So, what makes you think you're so different from some of the rest of us?" he asked.

I didn't understand at first, but then I realized that I wasn't the first person at the VOP to be criticized and accused. He was just telling me that such problems come with the territory.

During the 1970s someone began writing, making really serious accusations—saying I was having affairs with just about everyone under the sun. And they didn't send the letters just to me. They sent copies to the manager of the VOP, and even to church administrators back on the East Coast. But the worst thing was that one of the ministers at Church headquarters started taking the accusations seriously. He wrote a letter saying how serious these accusations were and that we needed to get to the bottom of it—kind of overdramatizing the situation.

I was so discouraged when I saw that letter, because it was at a time when I was putting forth special efforts to work with the young people in the church. I thought that letter was going to put an untimely end to that special mission. I can remember driving down the freeway one Sunday, actually hoping and praying that I'd have an accident that would affect only me and my life would be over. That's how bad I felt.

I was about as low as I've ever been in my life when I went into the office the following Monday morning. I was just sitting there with these dark thoughts running through my mind, thinking that my life was over, when I heard a knock on the door. I opened the door and there stood Pastor E. L. Minchin. He was a youth leader in our church, and I had worked with him many times as a singer for youth congresses. He had always impressed me as a truly godly man. He was known as a man who really walked with God.

Pastor Minchin said, "Del, may I come in? I was just leaving, and I had an inner voice telling me to go see Del. I'm wondering if you're OK."

I immediately dissolved in a flood of tears and told him that no, things were definitely not OK. I jerked some of the letters out of my file and let him read them.

After he read them, he looked at me and said, "Well, the Lord sent me up here for some reason, and I have to ask this. Is this true? If it is, I think that God wants me to tell you that He loves you and can forgive you."

I said, "Pastor Minchin, there isn't any truth to this at all. I'm just not that kind of a person!"

"Well, I didn't think so," he said. "But, I believe then the Lord sent me to your room here to tell you to leave your reputation up to Him." After that, he prayed with me, asking the Lord to help me through this time and to defend me from my accusers. Then he dashed out the door. He had a plane to catch, but he'd taken the time to stop by—in response to God's prompting—to help me.

After that, I was on cloud nine. As I look back over my life, I'd have to say that what had started out as one of my worst experiences ever turned into one of the best, not only because of Pastor Minchin's concern, but because it showed me how God works. That He was interested in me and how I was feeling. Interested enough to send one of His dedicated servants to help me through.

And I'm not special. I believe God is just that concerned about every one of His children here on earth. He doesn't always send someone to help out—I've gone through many difficult experiences when I didn't see His hand working so clearly. But I've always remembered that one experience, and it's helped me through other tough times. And as I've shared it with others, it's given them encouragement as well.

I think what Pastor Minchin did that day made a major impact on my life in another area as well. It taught me the value of speaking an encouraging word when it's needed—and being there for my friends when they hit rough spots on their journey.

That lesson came home to me very powerfully—and literally—on one of the most fascinating journeys I've ever had the privilege of making.

Chapter Thirteen

"Have you received any letters from Washington, D.C., lately?" The Chief asked me one day in the spring of 1951. There was a twinkle in his eye, so I had a feeling he knew something I didn't know.

H. M. S. Richards, Sr., had a reputation as a great Bible student, evangelist, pastor, and, of course, radio preacher. People all over the country recognized his dramatic voice proclaiming the soon coming of Jesus. So most people think he was probably pretty serious all the time—always had his nose in a book or thinking some deep, serious thoughts. And, of course, there was that side to him. Early in my years at the VOP I would sometimes travel to appointments with him and the King's Heralds. The Chief would always sit in the front beside the driver with a box of books. He could read for hours, but then when he'd get tired of reading, he'd lean back a bit and talk to us, sharing things he'd learned, or just tell funny stories of things that had happened to him through the years.

He wasn't the type to be silly, but he definitely had a strong sense of humor. One of his favorite sayings was "God Himself must have a sense of humor; otherwise He wouldn't have made monkeys and people!"

So, when The Chief stopped me in the hall and I saw that twinkle in his eye, I knew there must be something going on that he was party to. But I'd just have to wait until the letter came from Washington to find out what. He himself had just returned from attending some meetings at our Church's world headquarters there in Washington.

I didn't have long to wait. When I got home that evening, there was a letter with a Washington, D.C., postmark. It was from my friend Leona Running.

When I first came to the VOP, Leona had worked in the language department. She's a few years older than I am and had been married, but her husband had died several years before. Because of the age difference, we hadn't done a lot together while we worked at the VOP, but we had gotten acquainted. I wondered what in the world she could be writing to me about—it must be something important, because The Chief had known about it before the letter even came.

I opened the envelope with trembling hands. In a brief letter, Leona explained that she had always dreamed of taking a trip to Europe, and that for the past several months she had been saving and planning for a journey that would include a visit to a European youth congress meeting in Paris, France, July 24-29. She said that she and a young college woman had made all the arrangements, even buying their steamer tickets for the trip to Europe, but that her friend had suddenly decided to get married that summer instead of going to Europe.

The upshot was that Leona had an extra round-trip steamer ticket, and she wondered whether I might want to buy it and join her on a five-week trip through seven countries of Europe.

What a dream come true that would be! I was so excited at the thought that I could hardly breathe for a few minutes. Imagine— seeing Big Ben, the Eiffel Tower, the Louvre, the Colosseum. It would be the adventure of a lifetime. Of course I wanted to go with her! I was ready to run right down to the telegraph office and send her the message, "Count me in!"

But then reality began to settle in.

Where would I get the money for such a trip? Just the steamer ticket would take a big chunk out of my meager savings account.

Chapter Thirteen

And of course there would be hotels, train tickets, and a host of other expenses. Yes, it was nice to dream. But I knew there was no way that I could afford to fulfill the dream.

The next day when The Chief saw me, he asked again whether I'd gotten the letter from Washington. I smiled. "Yes. Leona invited me to travel to Europe with her. That would be so neat. But . . . "

"I knew she was going to invite you," he said. "So, are you going to go?"

"I'd love to. But there's no way I can afford it."

"Didn't I ever tell you that God has a thousand ways to provide for us that we know nothing of?" he asked.

"Yes, I've heard you say that."

"Well," he said. "You know my wife, Mabel, don't you?"

"Yes, of course."

"Well, she's been bothering me about something for quite a while. She says we've been working you too hard, Del, and I've noticed that too. You're always here, every day faithful as Big Ben's bell. And then we send you out traveling almost every weekend and sometimes in the evening too. Mabel noticed you've been looking a little tired lately. Have you been feeling OK?"

I assured The Chief that I was all right, but admitted that I had indeed been feeling a bit overworked.

"Well, Mabel and I really appreciate everything you do, Del," Pastor Richards said. "I think you ought to give Mabel a ring on the telephone when you get a chance. She's been cooking up something that I think you just might be interested in."

"Really? What's . . ." I started to ask what it was, but he just smiled and went on his way.

I hurried right back to my office and called Mrs. Richards at home. She inquired as to how I was feeling and told me how much she appreciated all that I had been doing lately and asked if I thought I could stand to take a little break from my hectic schedule. I admitted that I could indeed stand a break, and that's when she told me that The Chief had told her about the invitation coming from Leona. "I really think you ought to take that trip. It'll do you good, don't you think?" she asked.

"I'd love to, Mrs. Richards," I said. "But there's just no way I could afford it."

"Oh, yes there is," she said. "I've been asking around a little, and a lot of your friends, and even some people you don't know, have all chipped in. I've got a little monetary gift for you over here at the house. I think it'll be quite enough to assure a really pleasant trip to Europe for you."

I could hardly believe what I was hearing.

But that was so much like Pastor and Mrs. Richards. They were so concerned for everyone that they met—and especially for the staff members at the VOP. The Chief had known that I'd had an invitation to sing at the youth congress in Paris, and that I had desperately wished that there could be some way that I could fulfill that request, but hadn't dared to dream that it really could be possible. When he'd seen Leona in Washington, she'd told him about her dilemma since her intended companion had dropped out, and he'd told her to write to me and invite me to go with her. Then, as soon as he'd gotten home, he'd gone about—with Mabel's help—making sure that I'd be able to accept the invitation when it came.

It reminds me of a favorite quotation that The Chief liked to cite from the book *Christ's Object Lessons:* "All His biddings are enablings." When he and Mabel found out about my opportunity, they didn't just leave me to my own devising—they set about to enable me to fulfill my dream.

It took a few minutes for the reality of the good news to sink in, but when it did, I hurried right over to the telegraph office and sent a message to Leona: "You have got yourself a traveling pal!"

I had about two months to plan and get ready for the trip, and I set to it with gusto. The very opportunity to go had helped me see the value of taking an interest in others and helping them out. Events on the trip would reinforce that important perspective.

Chapter Fourteen

On Tuesday, July 3, 1951, I boarded an airplane in Los Angeles, bound for New York. That's where I met up with Leona, and we were able to spend the fourth and fifth seeing the sights of America's largest city before boarding the S. S. Veendam, a Holland-America passenger ship bound for Southampton, England. That ship was our home for the next ten days as we crossed the Atlantic. We had booked ourselves into a tourist class stateroom, but before we boarded we were fortunate to meet quite a few other Seventh-day Adventists who were heading to Europe on the same ship. Since some of them were traveling first class, we had the opportunity—at their invitation—to visit the first-class quarters as well as the tourist-class area we had booked passage in. One thing we noticed was that many people from first class liked to visit the tourist-class lounges, because things were more relaxed and less formal there.

The trip was largely uneventful, but one acquaintance I made stands out in my memory. Shorty was a middle-aged man who seemed to be everybody's friend and the life of the party. One day, as I was sitting on the deck, he came by and struck up a conversation. It wasn't long before I could tell that all the joking and frivolity was just a mask he was wearing, hiding something inside that he didn't want others to know about. For some reason he felt comfortable opening up to me, and I learned that he was hurting badly. His beloved wife had died not many months before, and he was doing his best to get on with life, but his sorrow was still very deep and very real.

I told him I'd like to share something from the Bible with him, if he was interested. He said sure, he'd be glad to listen, so I opened to Daniel 2 and shared with him the hope of the Second Coming.

He seemed to really appreciate it and promised to read his own Bible, and to listen to *The Voice of Prophecy* on Sunday mornings when he returned to the United States. The last Sunday of the cruise, a Dutch minister held a worship service and asked me to sing a solo. I noticed that Shorty was there, and I had him in mind when I was deciding what to sing. He seemed to be deeply moved by the song "I'd Rather Have Jesus."

On Monday, July 16, our ship pulled into port in Southampton, England. What a thrill we felt as we hurried ashore and boarded a train headed for London.

During the Atlantic crossing, we'd had plenty of time to review the itinerary plans Leona had so meticulously laid out as she tried to harmonize her aspirations to see as much of Europe as possible with the travel budget she had allowed herself. It was possible to travel very inexpensively in Europe in those days—travel books suggested that ten dollars a day was a reasonable budget for the economy-minded traveler! But of course a dollar was a lot harder to come by in those days too, and both of us were living on pretty meager secretarial wages.

Still, as we reviewed the planned itinerary, I felt like something was missing. Leona had four main destinations in mind—places she just had to see on this, her first trip to Europe. The first, of course was "Merry England," including London and Shakespeare country. Next, she wanted to be sure to have a steamer ride on the Rhine River in Germany, where one can see many castles and review much of the mythology and history of Germany. Of course, the next thing on her itinerary would be the youth congress in Paris, which was to begin just eight days after our arrival in England, and would last for six days. She figured we'd have some time to see the highlights of Paris during the congress; then we'd head for Switzerland, spend some time in the Alps, and visit a college our denomination owns at Collonges, just across the border from Geneva. That would just about use up our three-and-one-half weeks in Europe. We had return trip tickets for departure from France on August 8.

On our final review of the itinerary before disembarking, I realized what was missing. "Don't you want to go to Rome?" I asked. "What's a trip to Europe without seeing Rome? You're such a student of history; surely you want to go there, don't you?"

"Of course I'd like to tour Italy, but there's just no time. I'm afraid I've crammed everything into this trip that's humanly possible. I don't want to be rushing from one place to another so fast that I don't have time to really enjoy anything," she responded.

We went over the planned stops again, and I had to agree with her that she had filled the allotted time pretty well. But I still wanted to go to Rome. "Do you think we could possibly extend our trip a little—maybe get a later ship on the return—and give ourselves a couple of extra days?" I asked.

We decided it was certainly worth checking into, so on our first day in London, we made inquiries at the Holland-America office, only to discover that the first ship with any vacancies wouldn't be heading for America until November. And the ticket agent assured us that the same was the case with all the shipping lines. Everyone had drawers full of names of people hoping for a berth. There was just no hope of booking a later passage that would fit within the time frame of the leaves of absence we had from our jobs.

I've been told, once or twice, that I'm kind of stubborn. Well, I prefer to call it perseverance. I believe that if you want to do something bad enough, you ought to keep trying until you succeed, or figure out that it's just not going to be possible. So, even though we took the time to confirm our return passage at the Holland-America office, my mind didn't rest. Later that day I shared a new inspiration with Leona—what would happen if, instead of returning by ship, we flew? Instead of spending ten days crossing the Atlantic, we could do it in one, and that would give us plenty of time to visit Rome and other places in Italy.

At first Leona just looked at me like I was crazy, but the more she thought about it, the better it sounded to her. She really did like the idea of seeing Rome. Finally she said, "Oh, well, what's a travel budget, anyhow? Let's look into it."

We hurried right down to the American Express office and made inquiries. It would cost a lot more to fly—in fact, the difference in the ticket prices would use up most of Leona's planned travel budget—but still it seemed appealing. We told the American Express agent to make a tentative reservation. We'd sleep on it.

The next morning the prospects of a longer stay in Europe seemed even more alluring, and we hurried back to American Express and arranged for the refund of our ship tickets and the purchase of tickets on TWA for a flight to New York from Paris on August 20. That would give us thirteen extra days in Europe, and still get us back home within a couple days of when we had planned to arrive.

In those days before plastic money, a change like that involved further complications as well. We would need a new infusion of cash to see us through our journey, so we each wired home. My money arrived at American Express a couple of days later, but Leona's never caught up with her. But that was no problem. I had requested enough to meet the needs of two frugal travelers if all went well.

With our return arrangements cared for, we set out on three wonderful days of touring England. From there we flew to Brussels, Belgium, where we toured for one day before boarding a train for Holland. Just as we were going through the ticket gate on our way to the train, I had a sudden sense that something was not right. My purse seemed lighter than it ought to be. Hurriedly I looked through it and discovered that my precious travel diary—which contained not only my notes from the trip so far, but the names and addresses of many people whom I had talked to and had promised to send free Bible lessons—was missing.

I had written some notes in the diary that morning in our hotel lobby, so I knew I must have left it there. Glancing at my watch, I realized that I had just enough time to get a taxi, go back, retrieve the diary, and still make this train. And if that didn't work out, we could always take the next train to Amsterdam.

Chapter Fourteen

Leona agreed to wait there with the luggage while I hurried back to the hotel. But I soon discovered that getting out of a European train station was no easy task. I rushed back to the place where attendants were punching tickets for people as they entered the station, but each time I would try to squeeze through, the agent would motion to me that I couldn't go through that way. Finally I spotted a police station and ran down there, but pounding on the windows and doors only proved that there was no one there.

Then I spotted him. My angel in white. I don't know that he was really an angel, but he sure acted like one. He was a vendor, selling refreshments from a little cart. I rushed over to him and was delighted to discover that he understood English. When I explained my predicament, he immediately closed up shop, allowing his customers to go to his competitor's stand nearby, then helped me procure a pass that would allow me to leave the station and return. Then he showed me to a gate and took me out and found a taxi, explaining to the driver what I needed. As he put me into the taxi, he told the driver to bring me right back there after we'd been to the hotel. "I'll be waiting for you right here," he assured me.

It took me only a moment at the hotel to recover my precious diary, and the driver quickly returned me to the station. There stood my angel, waiting for me. I hastily pulled a few dollars from my purse to give to him, but he waved me off, saying he didn't expect anything for his trouble. Only on my firm assistance would he accept two dollars to make up for the sales he had missed while helping me.

Fortunately we made it onto the train for Amsterdam. In Holland we enjoyed touring an island where the people still dress in their traditional costumes and carry on life much as it was lived a century before. That left us with just two days to get to Paris for the beginning of the youth congress. We wanted to fit the trip on the Rhine into that time, so we took a train down into Germany, going upstream beside the river part of the way, then got off at Bingen and took a steamer going downstream to Koblenz, viewing many castles and ruins along the way. From Koblenz we took a night train directly to Paris, arriving in time for the opening ceremonies on July 24.

I just can't describe how thrilling it was to meet with the thousands of young people from all over Europe at the historic youth congress. Remember, this was taking place just six years after the end of World War II. Leona and I were moved to tears more than once as we saw youth who had been born on opposite sides of battle and propaganda lines meeting, embracing, and sharing their common love for their Savior. Incidentally, the youth leader of the Northern European Division at that time was Pastor E. L. Minchin, who would play such an important part in my life more than twenty years later. The youth congress in Paris was my first acquaintance with this godly man. He often led the spirit-filled song services at the meeting.

Leona had thought that we could play hooky from the meetings and spend several half-days sightseeing in Paris during the congress, but both of us found the meetings and fellowship so inspiring that we couldn't bear to miss a moment. In Europe *The Voice of Prophecy* broadcast is called *Voice of Hope,* and we were especially excited to get acquainted with the staff of both the German and French broadcasts.

One of the highlights of any meeting like this is usually a mission pageant, when young people from the various conferences come in their ancestral costumes and put on a parade and give their testimonies. The pageant was scheduled for Saturday afternoon, and I was honored to be able to have a part, representing the United States and The Voice of Prophecy by singing two solos during the program.

When the congress ended the next day, we felt like the highlight of our whole trip was over. Sorrowfully we bid farewell to dozens of new friends we had made, but with a firm hope in our hearts that even if we never again met on this earth, we'd all be a part of a wonderful, eternal youth congress in heaven one day soon.

Chapter Fifteen

Since we hadn't taken any time out for tourist activities during the youth congress, Leona and I decided to spend the Monday and Tuesday after the meetings ended touring Paris. And we also expected to have a few days for seeing that great cosmopolitan city at the end of our trip, since our flight was scheduled to depart from there on August 20. On Monday morning we walked down the Champs-Elysées, and in the afternoon took a bus tour to the famous palace at Versailles.

On Tuesday morning, we decided to forego further sightseeing in favor of a visit to the Voice of Hope studios. We found our friends from the German Voice of Hope quartet in the studio, recording songs for the next year's broadcast, and were even able to help them in assembling their program. After lunch with the broadcast staff, we spent the afternoon seeing Notre Dame cathedral and other Parisian high points. By the time we arrived at the Eiffel Tower, the upper levels were closed, but we were able to go as high as the second level. From there it was possible to see almost all of Paris, since the city had no buildings over nine stories tall to block our view.

Early Wednesday morning, we boarded a train for Geneva, Switzerland, unwittingly arriving there in the midst of one of their greatest holidays, the equivalent of America's Fourth of July. By the time we found a hotel and climbed the stairs to the sixth floor (fourth floor by European reckoning, which doesn't count the first floor and mezzanine), we were exhausted and flopped into bed, only to be awakened an hour or so later by the sound of firecrackers going off all over the city.

All together we were able to spend nearly a week enjoying the sights in Switzerland and also crossed over into France long enough to visit our church's college at Collonges. On Sabbath we attended church in Bern, and I was requested to sing during the worship service. The following Wednesday, the very day when we would have had to board a ship for the return to America, had we not changed our plans, we instead boarded a train bound for Rome!

The Eternal City was all we expected it to be. We were able to visit Vatican City, see St. Peter's Cathedral, the Sistine Chapel, the Basilica of St. Paul, the Colosseum, the Roman Forum, the Mammertine Prison, and countless other sites we had dreamed of seeing. After three days in Rome, we headed farther south, for we wanted to visit Pompeii, the ancient city destroyed by a volcano in A.D. 79. The scenes we witnessed there left us feeling somber, thinking about the final judgment and wondering how many of the residents had been prepared to face the end of their lives that day.

While in Switzerland we had been invited to lunch by Pastor and Mrs. W. R. Beach. Our hostess had told us that since we were going to Italy, we simply must visit the island of Capri and the Blue Grotto, so we arranged for a car to take us to the dock where we could catch the boat. After that, it was time to begin our return train trip to Paris.

When I first told one of my friends at the VOP that I was going to take a month-long trip through Europe with Leona, my friend just shook her head and said, "Good luck! I'll bet by the end of the trip the two of you will never speak to each other again!"

Well, we were determined that that would not happen. And we traveled really well together, despite the fact that by nature we're quite opposites in many ways. As I mentioned before, I'm a night person and Leona is a morning person. We were also quite different in the way we responded to schedules—I wanted to be at the train station way in advance, while Leona tended to arrive at the last minute. But perhaps that worked out for the better—often our trains departed early in the morning, so our contrasting personalities worked together—she, the morning person got us up early enough, and I usually made sure we were at the station with time to spare. "Just stick with me," I told her, "And you'll never miss a train."

And my words had proven true, even when I'd had to dash back to the hotel in Brussels to get my diary. But needless to say, after so much traveling together, no matter how amiable the companions, there come times when differing personalities begin to rub the wrong way on each other.

Maybe that's what was going on the next day back in Rome, as we made our way through the train station. Leona remembers looking back at me, trailing a bit behind her at the moment, and pointing to my purse, which I had neglected to zip completely closed after extracting my ticket as we hurried into the station. Leona said, "It drives me crazy to see you go along with that purse open."

I guess I wasn't in the best of moods so early in the morning. Anyhow, she remembers that I kind of snapped back at her, "Oh, you let too many things drive you crazy!"

Those were probably just about the only sharp words that passed between us the whole time, but boy would I have opportunity to regret my cockiness a bit later!

The train ride to Nice, on the south coast of France, took thirteen hours, and we arrived after dark, only to discover that all the hotels were full because the next day was a holiday. I stayed at the railroad station while Leona went looking for a place to spend the night. When she returned with the news that there wasn't a room to be had anywhere in the city, we hastily decided that our only option was to take the night train to Paris. We got tickets on the 9:40 train, and I quickly handed Leona some money to go get us some food to eat along the way and carefully placed my passport wallet back in my purse.

Was I being recalcitrant when I didn't zip it up—just showing her that I was a big girl that didn't have to let her worries bother me—or was I just too tired to care? I don't know. But when we got onto the train, I suddenly noticed that once again my purse was lighter than it should have been. This time it wasn't my diary that was missing, but my passport wallet—with all my traveler's checks, my cash, and worst of all, my passport!

The next eighteen hours were a hectic, befuddled, stressful time as we tried our best to get help from the local police and find a place to stay. Fortunately, we finally caught the attention of the chief of police, who helped us find a room, transported us from place to place, and filed the report of the lost items.

The only cash we had was a bit of change, since Leona had been relying on me for her supply because the money she had requested to be wired to her had never caught up with us. The few coins and bills we had between us proved adequate for only one night's stay in Nice, so the next day we used our train tickets to take us to Paris, where we would be able to get a cash advance from our local church headquarters.

The thing I most remember about that difficult time is how kind and patient Leona was with me. She never once said, "See, I told you that you should have zipped up your purse!" She stuck with me, buoying me up when I was too tired and discouraged to go on. This time she was my angel, helping me out when I needed it most.

In Paris I was able to go to the American embassy and apply for a duplicate passport, but when we went to the American Express office later, we learned that my wallet had been recovered by the police in Nice. My passport was in it, but every bit of money had been removed—even a tiny Dutch coin I had kept as a souvenir.

When the dust finally settled from my wallet fiasco, we had two more days that we spent sightseeing in Paris; then we boarded a TWA Constellation for the long flight home.

Much of my life since then seems to have involved travel. Sometimes I think I've spent more time living out of a suitcase than living at home. But the memories of that trip with Leona, and the precious lessons that were reinforced in my mind—about being a helper to those in need—make it one of my fondest travel memories.

Chapter Sixteen

In 1952 I decided that it was time to fulfill my long-delayed dream of attending college. One of the reasons that I had turned down the call to come to the VOP the first three times I was contacted in 1947 was that I just didn't feel qualified. I had only a high-school education, and I hadn't had any formal music training. So, finally, after singing and working for five years, I decided it was time for me to go and get the education I had always longed for.

At first The Chief did not want me to go to college because he was afraid I would be influenced to change my musical style and sing just classical music. He knew that our simple songs about Jesus touched the hearts of our listeners in a very special way. I assured him that I was taking a religion major and would not forget how to sing simple gospel songs and hymns. (Actually, the quartet and I used a variety of styles in our music ministry through the years.)

He remained unconvinced for quite a while, but then my boss, Bessie Flaiz-Detamore spoke up and reminded him that all of his children, including his daughter, had attended college, and none of them had been ruined by the experience! Incidentally, The Chief's children and grandchildren have all been good friends of mine through the years. I'll have a lot to say about Harold (H. M. S. Richards, Jr.) later, but right now let me mention that two of the finest people I know are Kenneth and Jackie Richards. Kenneth is the second son of The Chief and Mabel. Ken was a pastor for years and then joined the VOP as a scriptwriter and announcer. He has his doctorate in Old Testament exegesis. (I never call Ken "Dr. Richards"—I tease him that I want him to remain level-headed!) Jackie was our switchboard operator for quite some time. The next son, Jan, is the baby of the family. He teaches philosophy and I hear that students clamor to be in his class. Then there's the smartest in the family (I say she's the smartest, because she's a woman!), who is also the oldest, Virginia Cason. She and her physician husband, Walt, are retired now, but before retirement she was very much in demand as a speaker.

It didn't take much more persuasion to win The Chief over. Finally he agreed that I should go to college—not that his lack of support would actually have prevented me from going. When I decide I'm going to do something, it takes a lot to stop me.

There were a number of suitable colleges in California, but Dr. Percy Christian, the president of Emmanuel Missionary College (EMC—now Andrews University) up in Michigan, was the one who got my attention. He promised me a partial scholarship to help with my expenses if I would come to his school.

So in September 1953, I took a leave of absence from the VOP, packed my bags, left the palm trees and balmy breezes of Southern California behind, and headed for Michigan. I may have been born in South Dakota, but that doesn't mean I like the climate up north! I'm definitely a warm-weather person, and I didn't have any romantic dreams of snowball fights or slalom skiing. I like to ski, I'll grant you that, but the kind I like is the kind you do behind a boat when it's ninety degrees outside.

The June 1954 Voice of Prophecy newsletter took a retrospective look at my first year in college with this brief report:

> School bells rang last September for Del Delker, contralto on *The Voice of Prophecy* broadcast. But before she left our office for Emmanuel Missionary College in Michigan, she made a series of recordings for Voice of Prophecy programs.

During the school year she frequently interrupted her class work to witness for Christ in sacred concerts, evangelistic rallies, and youth meetings throughout the eastern United States and Canada. As the school year ends, The Voice of Prophecy staff welcomes her back to a very busy schedule here in the West.

There was a lot more to it than that, though. I had been singing on the radio for long enough by then that I had a definite celebrity status (not that I have ever felt like a celebrity, but that's the way they looked at me), especially among Adventists. Remember, this was in the days when television wasn't yet widely available in rural areas, and even if it had been, most conservative Christians wouldn't consider having a set in their homes. Many probably still considered radio a tool of the devil, and if they listened at all, it was only to religious programs. So TV must certainly be doubly cursed!

And there weren't a whole lot of Christian programs on the air in those days. The book *The Churching of America, 1776-1990* by Roger Finke and Rodney Stark reports that during the 1930s and '40s, the Federal Council of Churches (later National Council of Churches) persuaded most of the networks not to sell air time for religious broadcasts to churches not affiliated with their organization. For most of those decades only the Mutual Broadcasting System would sell time to evangelical Christians. The authors note that "even with this limited access the evangelicals produced the most popular religious shows on radio: Charles E. Fuller's 'Old Fashioned Revival Hour'; 'The Lutheran Hour,' sponsored by the Missouri Synod Lutherans, and the 'Voice of Prophecy' which was produced by Seventh-day Adventists. These shows attracted millions of listeners." *

In 1949, the ABC network began to carry our program as well, and throughout most of the '50s and into the '60s, we were carried coast to coast on both ABC and Mutual. (Later, we were also on NBC for several years.) That meant that we were heard almost ev-

---

*(New Brunswick: Rutgers University Press, 1992), 219.

erywhere in the U. S., and the program was also carried overseas. In Central and South America and several countries in Europe there were locally produced broadcasts, but guess who did the music for those! In fact, almost everywhere in the world you could hear *The Voice of Prophecy* (or *Voice of Hope* as the program is called in most non-English-speaking areas) in a local language, and for the most part the music for these programs came directly from our studios in Glendale, California. Even countries that formed their own quartets often used me as their female soloist. Through the years the King's Heralds and I recorded music in fifteen different languages including Arabic, German, Ukrainian, Vietnamese, Chinese, Indonesian, and two Philippine dialects for use on broadcasts produced in far corners of the world.

I think that Adventists by and large regarded the VOP as the fulfillment of Matthew 24:14 and Revelation 14:6, which predict that the gospel will be preached "in all the world for a witness unto all the nations" and "to every nation, tribe, tongue, and people" just before the Second Coming. As a result, H. M. S. Richards, his associate speakers, and we musicians were regarded as celebrities, whether we liked it or not—especially among Adventists. During World War II and the years immediately following, Pastor Richards and the quartet traveled all across North America, speaking and singing at camp meetings, on college campuses, and in evangelistic meetings. The best car they could find for that purpose in those days was an old 1938 Cadillac limousine that they purchased from a well-known film actress Dolores del Rio. Imagine the excitement generated on an Adventist campus when that big, black car pulled in and the world-famous speaker and quartet emerged. Often there would be a crowd of young people waiting at the entrance to see who could catch the first glimpse of the car coming, and they would throng around, running along behind as the touring group pulled into the campground or campus. An article published in the VOP monthly paper at the end of 1952 told about the group's fourth tour of the summer and reported that now all four of the quartet members had been to all forty-eight states. That's quite an accomplishment, considering that this group had only been together since 1949! Virtually all of this

Chapter Sixteen

travel was done by car, and remember the Interstate freeway system hadn't been built yet.

These men drew the same sort of enthusiastic crowds as a major television or movie star would today. And by 1953 much of that kind of aura had rubbed off on me. I had even been featured in several television productions produced for the new *Faith For Today* program by the VOP for broadcast on the West Coast. I can honestly say that I never sought or expected to be regarded as a celebrity, but as The Chief would say, it comes with the territory!

But celebrity wasn't exactly an asset when I arrived on the campus of Emmanuel Missionary College, out in the rolling countryside of southwestern Michigan in the fall of 1953. The girls in the dorm had me pegged long before I set foot on campus. They knew I'd be snooty and stuck up. Worse yet, I was probably a Holy Josephine who would spoil their fun by always quoting Bible texts at them to get them straightened out. So they figured they'd just give me the cold shoulder and teach me that I wasn't anyone special there. It's not that they were trying to be mean or anything, they just made some assumptions about me that I needed to prove wrong.

After enduring a few days of isolation, watching girls whisper about me when I walked past them in the dorm, I hit on a plan—an old joke that girls used to play on each other in high school. All it required was a little Vaseline and a toilet seat.

One night after things had pretty well quieted down in the dorm, I sneaked out of my room and applied my magic potion to the seat in a room where the girls had been particularly cool toward me. When word got out about it, the buzz went up and down the hall two or three times—who could have pulled that stunt? When they found out that it was the famous (now infamous) Del Delker, everyone was amazed. Could it be that this high-falutin' Holy Josephine radio star was just a normal young woman who enjoyed a good joke as much as the next person?

A few of the girls decided to find out, and it wasn't long before I had made many new friends. Being in my late twenties, I was quite a bit older than most of my dorm mates, and I had to work a lot plus attend classes and contribute to various musical programs, so I didn't have time to socialize as much as I might have a few years earlier. But I was glad that the girls began to see me as a normal human being, who wasn't going to try to use my well-known name to get special treatment.

Once the girls began to accept me as part of their group, I was able to begin to minister to them spiritually as well. One of the things I did was start a prayer group. Several of us would meet in my dorm room to pray about special needs and study the Bible together. That's probably why they brought Susan (not her real name) to me. She and her parents had only recently become Christians, and they'd come out of a spiritualistic background. Susan seemed like a normal girl most of the time, but then all of a sudden, without warning, a dark power would come over her, and she'd start making odd sounds and saying very negative things. Her friends became concerned that maybe Satan was trying to take over her life again, despite the fact her devil-worshiping days were behind her.

It was a moving moment when half a dozen of us dorm mates gathered in a little circle around Susan and united our voices in prayer, asking Jesus to come in and take control of Susan's life and keep the devil away.

There was no dramatic deliverance like you sometimes read about, with the devil speaking through her or anything like that. But there was a deliverance nonetheless. Susan left that room with a sweet, serene smile on her face and to my knowledge was never again troubled by demonic powers. There had been a titanic struggle going on for that girl's soul, and I was just happy that the other members of the prayer group and I were able to take the Lord's side and help her find deliverance.

I didn't learn about it until later, but my arrival on campus contributed to another kind of struggle as well. This one was in the music department.

Pastor Richards had been afraid for me to go to college for fear that the musicians there would try to change me and turn me into a classical musician unable to do the simple gospel songs that our audience loved so much. Well, the distrust between musical styles went the other direction as well. Melvin Davis was in charge of the choir in those days, and I was told by another faculty member that Melvin was determined that I wasn't going to be a part of his choir or of his special musical group known as The Collegians. He evidently thought I considered myself a celebrity and would want more than my share of the solos.

But the president of the college had given me a partial scholarship with the understanding that I would indeed represent the school in their musical programs. Well, of course, a president outranks a department head, so I soon found myself being invited to join The Collegians.

Boy was Mr. Davis surprised the first time he asked me to do a solo. I flat out refused. I had no desire at all to push myself to the forefront. Finally he came to me and practically begged me to do a solo, and I consented. I guess that helped to change his opinion of me, because we soon became good friends, and remained so until his death.

My days at EMC were some of the busiest, yet most enjoyable, of my life (when I wasn't hiking through blizzards and three-foot snowdrifts on the way to class, that is!). I worked several hours each weekday as a secretary for Professor Horace Shaw, head of the speech department, attended classes, of course, and spent many weekends off campus traveling with The Collegians or taking appointments for the VOP.

Being kept so busy didn't discourage me. I was excited that I had made a good first step toward earning a college diploma, and I left the campus that spring intending to return in the fall. But a pair of eyes would change all that.

Chapter Seventeen

I received a warm welcome back at the VOP after my year at EMC. Not long after I returned, The Chief dropped by my office one day to see how things were going. After a little catching up, he paused for a moment and said, "Del, I can understand why you want to go to college, and I'm glad you do. I'm proud of you for what you're doing, and I want to apologize for not backing you up when you first said you wanted to go."

After I thanked him for his kind words, he said, "I was just wondering though, why you chose to go clear back to Michigan. Isn't there a college here in California that you could attend? That way we'd have you closer by, and maybe you could even come over and record a few songs for us once in a while and go with some of us on our weekend appointments."

My heart was set on going back to EMC, where I had made so many new friends. But when he looked at me with those big, brown cocker-spaniel eyes (he actually had only one good eye, but that didn't stop him from turning on the charm!), well, I just couldn't turn him down. I promised to at least look into the possibility of continuing my education in California.

That's how I ended up at La Sierra College near Riverside, California, in the fall of 1954. It must have seemed odd to the eighteen- and nineteen-year-old freshmen arriving on campus to find a thirty-year-old radio singer living in the dorm with them. Most people my age probably would have wanted to have their own private apartment. But I'd learned an important lesson fairly early in my ministry with the VOP.

At first it didn't come naturally to me to spend much time mingling with people at meetings I attended. I was very shy and didn't know what to say. I'd sing my songs, then sit down, and when the meeting was over, I'd be looking for the exit. But a couple of years before I went to La Sierra, I traveled a bit with Beth Thurston, who had replaced Al Avila as the organist for the broadcast in 1952. Beth somehow understood what it took to make sure music had its full impact on people, and she pulled me aside. "You shouldn't go dashing out after the meeting," she counseled me. "You'll never win the hearts of the people that way. You need to rub shoulders with them. Visit with the ones who come down to the front at the end of the meeting. Pray with those who have a special need."

I took her counsel to heart and found that she was right. People really appreciated the personal touch as well as the onstage appearance. Soon I was spending more time ministering to people on a one-to-one basis than I was spending singing.

And that was one of the things I looked forward to at college as well. I figured that if I lived off campus, I wouldn't have much chance to get to know the other students. So I moved into the dorm. One of my roommates there was Sonja Rust (now Nicola). She likes to remind me of a few of the antics I pulled there, like bringing a frog into the dorm and dropping it on a friend's stomach while she was engrossed in reading a book on her bed. Once again, innocent pranks helped me find acceptance among the other students. But then there was the time we were returning to campus after meeting an appointment somewhere. It was late at night and I was tired, and I guess I rolled slowly through an intersection with a stop sign without coming to a full stop. Sonja asked, "Didn't you see that stop sign?"

"Oh, didn't you notice?" I joked. "It said Pause, not Stop!" We were having a good laugh about that when I noticed the red light flashing in my rearview mirror. I pulled over to the side of the road, and the policeman came around and stopped in front of me. I got out of the car to go talk to him, and believe me it didn't make matters any better for me when I neglected to set the parking brake and my car rolled slowly forward and bumped his car. Fortunately no damage was done to either vehicle, but there was certainly no possibility I could talk my way out of a ticket after that! Sonja was a fabulous roommate. The only thing I had against her was that she was smarter than I! She didn't have to study nearly as hard as I did. After all these years we are still very dear friends.

Sonja's mother Violet was a Truman. Violet's father, Dr. A. W. Truman, was medical secretary of the General Conference of Seventh-day Adventists. Dr. Truman was a cousin of President Harry Truman. Are you impressed? I actually roomed with a relative of a former president!

I had another roommate at La Sierra named Nellie Bray (now Kimbrough). She is also a brilliant and happy-go-lucky, fun person. I got some of the same grades as those girls got, but I had to work twice as hard to get them—what a humbling experience!

One of the reasons I hadn't wanted to go to La Sierra in the first place was that somehow I had gotten the impression that it was a very worldly place without much Christian influence. But it turned out that I was wrong about that, and I ended up enjoying my years there just as much as I'd enjoyed the year at EMC. I found a lot of spiritually-minded people to associate with and started a prayer group in my dorm room again.

I majored in religion, which meant that I took many of my classes with the ministerial students. Now, you might think that there was a plan behind that—maybe I was hoping to fulfill my earlier dream of meeting a ministerial student and settling down to a quiet life as a pastor's wife.

I can't say that the thought never crossed my mind. There were quite a few nice fellows that I dated off and on during my college years. But many of them shied away after a while, realizing that my well-known name would be a problem to them. Others seemed interested in me primarily because of my name, and that didn't provide much of a basis on which to build a serious relationship.

The real reason I took religion, though, wasn't social. I wanted to know that great Book better, so I could help others understand it and find God's answers to their problems. Along with my Bible major, I took a minor in counseling. I had noticed when I went out to sing that my music often touched the hearts of people with serious problems or special needs, and I wanted to do the best I could to help them when they came up to visit with me after the meeting. The things I learned while taking that minor in counseling have helped me through the years.

I was working toward a Bachelor of Arts degree, not a Bachelor of Science. But that didn't allow me to escape all the science classes. I'd never been very interested in, or good at, science in high school, so it was with fear and trepidation that I enrolled in Dr. Cushman's natural science class. I paid really close attention, even took down careful notes in shorthand and studied them religiously. But I guess when God made me, He left out the part of the brain that's supposed to understand science. Either that or some fool thing I did as a kid blocked the door to that part of my brain. I just couldn't seem to understand anything Dr. Cushman was talking about. After class one day, he pulled me aside to talk to me about my grade. The bad news was, there were quite a few students failing the class. The worse news was that most of them were musicians. And worse yet, I was one of them. The good news though, he told me, was that at that point I was at the top of the heap. Wow! I was the highest of the failures!

That news didn't make me feel a whole lot better, because in all the rest of my classes I was managing to pull very respectable grades and was even on the dean's list. I guess I must have redoubled my efforts after that little visit with Dr. C., because somehow I managed to pass the class, which was a requirement for graduation.

During all my time at college I continued to carry a fairly heavy schedule of VOP appointments on weekends, and, of course, in the summertime as well. In fact, there was one time when I found it necessary to drop out of classes for a short time to be able to do everything I felt I needed to do. But I managed to finish all my coursework in just four and one half years. Believe me, it was a very proud day when I finally marched down the aisle with my mortarboard and tassel at the beginning of the summer of 1958.

It was a short walk, compared to the other trips I was making in those days. But it was a very happy walk!

Chapter Eighteen

Ah, travel! It seems like such a glorious occupation! Just imagine if you could have a job that involved constantly going from place to place, meeting with large groups of people who adored you and always wanted you to sing them "just one more song!" Wouldn't it be fun?

I admit it sounds like fun when you first hear about it. And I guess that's actually the kind of life I dreamed of when I hoped to be a singer with a big band—although I don't think I had any conception of what was really involved when I cherished those girlish dreams.

Travel can be fun, and often is. But too much of a good thing can get old pretty fast. I'd like to give you a little glimpse of the kind of schedule that VOP traveling teams kept during the heavy travel season each summer, so I'm going to share an article I wrote for the VOP News in 1961. Notice that this article told only about our third tour of the summer. Prior to this itinerary, our group had made a three-and-a-half-week trip from California to Texas, Louisiana, Iowa, Wisconsin, Minnesota, North Dakota, Wyoming, and Idaho in May and June. Harold Richards (The Chief's son, H. M. S. Richards, Jr.) reported after this trip that he had preached thirty-one sermons on the twelve-stop tour that lasted twenty-five days.

"Group B"—Harold, the Braleys, and I, traveled all over the country together for many years. Harold always said B stood for Best!

Phyllis and Gordon Henderson were very active in evangelism. We traveled together to many places including South Africa.

Here I am with the King's Heralds, Harold, The Chief, and Jim Teel sometime in the late 1970s.

J. Orville Iverson, seated beside The Chief, was our announcer for many years. The Braleys and I traveled with him for several summers before the arrival of Harold Richards

In the 1960s we formed a group called "The Hymnsingers." It included the King's Heralds, plus Bunny Thornburgh and me, under the direction of Wayne Hooper.

In 1967 Harold Richards invited a little-known group called Wedgwood to travel to camp meetings with us. I really enjoyed singing folk music with them, and we even released an album together. Jerry Hoyle is on bass here, and Don Vollmer and Bob Summerour are playing guitars.

Wedgwood got together again for some reunion concerts a few years ago, and invited me to pose with them again.

I was honored to have the three fellows join me again for a number for the Del and Friends video in 2002.

Pastor Braulio Pérez-Marcio, center, founded La Voz de la Esperanza, the Spanish-language Voice of Prophecy. Not long after I arrived at VOP he had me singing in Spanish.

Of all the languages I learned to sing in, Vietnamese was certainly not the easiest. Here, Pastor Le Cong Giao is trying to prompt musical sounds in his language from the King's Heralds and me.

Pastor Wadie Farag was our coach when we sang in Arabic.

Through the years the King's Heralds Quartet has changed members from time to time. During my years with VOP I have sung with twelve different combinations. Most of the surviving members got together for a reunion concert in 2001, and invited me to join them for a song.

Children have always been important to me. Here's a group I sang to at a concert recently.

I first met Stephanie Dawn when she was four years old. She's a gospel singer now too.

Moses didn't like to listen to me at first. But - now he uses his musical talent to bless other children.

Kimberly asked, "May I kiss you?" I asked why. "Because I like you," she said.

Bernice Davidson was my close friend and roommate for many years.

Here's Bernice with her three daughters, Beth, Ann, and Carol.

VOP's Bible School staff really enjoyed working with Bernice. Only a few years after she started work there, she became the director of the school.

Bernice and I posed together in 1986 after I was named Woman of the Year by the Association of Adventist Women.

Our mutual friend Boleslaw was smart, but never could figure out how to get the girls to quit dressing her up like this!

A traveling we will go!
Much of my life has been spent on the road (read chapter 18). Here are some photos from the highlights of my travels.

Leona Running is on the left and I am on the right in this picture taken at the Paris youth congress in 1951.

I guess 1952 was a big year for travel, because here I am arriving in Hawaii with others from VOP for some meetings there later the same year.

I thought I'd surprise you and include a swimsuit picture. I think this was snapped while I was swimming in the Sea of Galilee during a Bible Lands tour with The Chief.

Boy do Harold and I know how to draw a crowd! Feeding the emus in Australia in 1986.

Our evangelism team in the Philippines in 1975. From left, Everett Tetz, Shirley Tetz, VOP's national speaker Pastor Galong, Fordyce Detamore, myself, and Calvin Taylor.

In Athens, Greece, probably on the same Holy Land tour.

I think New Zealand is one of the most beautiful places on earth. I was there with Harold Richards and Phil Draper in 1986.

We traveled with almost every imaginable form of conveyance in New Zealand and Australia. The Rolls was loaned to us.

Sometimes when you travel so much, you get to feeling about as energetic as a koala.

I didn't have to travel far when I was invited to sing at the Crystal Cathedral.

Evangelism was one of Harold Richards's favorite things. Here he and I are visiting with an interested woman at the entry to one of the air tents we used to set up for temporary meeting places.

The group that went to southern Brazil in 1993: Phil Draper, Jeannie and Lonnie Melashenko, and me.

The man in the foreground is evangelist and prayer warrior Glen Coon. Wayne Hooper and I were with him, but I'm not sure where the picture was taken.

Many of the miles I traveled were to large or small camp meetings and other church gatherings right here in North America. Here I'm singing to a group in Alberta, Canada.

Whenever I got to stay home, I carried on with secretarial responsibilities at VOP headquarters. I also got to play surrogate mom and guardian to a family of sparrows that nested on my windowsill.

I had my first hip surgery in the spring of 1969, and the King's Heralds came to visit me and sing to me.

An early studio recording session, after we moved into our new building in Glendale

Working with Calvin Taylor and Wayne Hooper to get an arrangement just right.

Orville Iverson, the Braleys, and I put on a lot of miles traveling to camp meetings all over the country.

Wherever I go, I like to spend some time with the children.

Phil Draper, Harold Richards, and I were a frequent traveling team during the 1980s.

Now it's usually Phil and VOP's current director-speaker Lonnie Melashenko, and me.

Sometimes I even let Lonnie sing with me!

And now for the obligatory celebrity encounter snapshots!

I met President Ferdinand Marcos of the Philippines when I visited Corregidor in 1975!

My good friend Phyllis chopped the top of Edgar Bergen's head off when she snapped this. Charlie McCarthy was sound asleep at the time.

Here I am with Desmond Doss, who was awarded the Congressional Medal of Honor for his heroism during World War II.

The honorable Jon Waihee, governor of Hawaii, attended a meeting where I sang in Honolulu.

On June 30, 2002, many of my friends joined me to tape a video program called Del and Friends. Here are a few pictures.

Chapter Eighteen

Then in July we had taken two camp meeting appointments in northern California—no short little jaunt in itself. A glance at a 1959 National Geographic map reveals that even in California there were very few freeways at that time. Most of our driving was done on two-lane roads replete with stop signs and stoplights in every small town.

Incidentally, our traveling troupe, which usually consisted of myself, keyboard artists Brad and Olive Braley, and an associate speaker, was formed in 1957 and given the title Group B. Group A, consisting of the Chief and the King's Heralds, carried on an equally strenuous itinerary. Nineteen sixty-one was the first year that Harold Richards headed up Group B. He always said B stood for Better!

Here's the account of Group B's third trip of the summer of '61. I called the article "More Miles for the Master," and it originally appeared in the October 1961 issue of *Voice of Prophecy News*.

Yes, 7,500 more miles for the Master on our third tour, making a total of 12,867 driven this summer of 1961. As we started this last tour, I thought out loud: "I wonder if we'll be doing this again next year." Olive Braley laughed and said, "You say that every year." Yes, I guess I did say it last year, and the year before—and the year before that. But this time I said it with more conviction than formerly. This year, with world conditions so much more serious than they have ever been in the past, I couldn't help wondering if God's work might not be finished and the second coming of our Lord Jesus Christ wouldn't be ushered in before we had a chance to go on another Voice of Prophecy trip. What a wonderful thought—but solemn, too.

I knew that many people would be coming to our meetings this summer who had never yet made a decision for Christ. Many would be there who had no idea that this life is just a sort of whistle stop in the immense circle of eternity. Many would be there whose hearts had been bruised and torn by sin or heartache, hearts that would need bandaging and comforting. It was our privilege, our great responsibility to be clear pipelines through which God could pour in His healing balm.

Our group was a little larger this trip. Along with Brad and Olive Braley, Pastor Harold Richards, and myself, there was Mary Margaret Richards, the vivacious, sagacious, and—well—just plain charming wife of Harold Richards. Although an extra passenger made the sides of our station wagon bulge just a little bit more, it was unanimously decided that the sparkle and joy she added to the trip more than compensated!

We didn't get off to a very good start. Scheduled departure time: August 2, 7:00 A. M. Actual departure time: August 3, 6:00 P. M. At the last minute, the Braleys' 1954 Chrysler New Yorker station wagon suffered a "nervous breakdown" in the form of valve trouble, and had to be sent to a car hospital for heavy "shock treatment" before we could take off. This late start inevitably made us late to our first appointment in Albuquerque, New Mexico. Friday night, August 4. We arrived at the church at 8:30 (after having traveled for almost 13 hours that day) in a hot, weary, rumpled condition. We heard singing coming from the church. Those poor people—at least some of them—had been there waiting for us since about 7:15! If this were not the church where Harold and Mary Margaret had spent three happy years pastoring before they came to the VOP, maybe most of the people would have gone back home and not waited so long. Mary helped Harold change clothes right out there in the parking lot of the church, while the rest of us dashed inside to throw clean clothes over our dirty bodies! And what wonderful fellowship we had with those fine Christian people that Friday night and all next day! After the Sabbath morning church service they took us out to the park for pot luck and fed us sumptuously. I enjoyed watching Harold and Mary cluck over their former parishioners like a couple of mother hens! Many of these people had been brought to Christ through their efforts. All true friends are fine, but there is something special about friendships in the Lord. "Blest be the tie that binds our hearts in Christian love! The fellowship of kindred minds is like to that above."

The next stop was Amarillo, Texas. The experience that stands out in my mind here is our visit to a rest home to "cheer up" a lady who, eleven years ago had been involved in a serious automobile accident, and was paralyzed from the waist down. Shortly after the accident her husband, deciding that he did not want to be tied to an invalid the rest of his life, deserted her and their small son. Almost five years ago a Christian nurse cared for her for a time, and led her to Christ and to a saving knowledge of His marvelous gospel of hope. This put a song in her heart and God's praise on her lips. You should see her radiant smile and hear her courageous testimony, in spite of the fact that it was necessary recently to amputate her legs. "Oh, don't worry about me!" she said cheerfully. "My body isn't in such good shape, but all is well with my soul. My only concern now is that my 14-year-old son will grow up to be a good Christian." "Who cheered whom?" we asked one another as we left! We all felt that we were the ones who had been cheered and encouraged!

On to Wichita Falls, Texas; Oklahoma City; and Enterprise, Kansas. It was music to our ears to hear person after person tell how God had captured their attention through the radio ministry. If you could have listened in on some of the conversations, you would have heard such as this: "As I was riding along one day in my car, I switched on the radio and got your broadcast. Little did I realize that this would start a chain of events that would bring me to the turning point in my life. Your Bible courses and radio ministry have introduced me to Christ, and now I am one of the happiest persons in the world."

Or you may have heard: "I'm so thankful that God has made it possible for His message of love and grace to go out over the air, so it would reach people like us who were without God and without hope. Please take our thanks to everyone who has a part in making this radio ministry possible." (And those thanks go to you and you and you who read these lines right now. You have prayed and given so faithfully and generously through the years, to sustain these broadcasts.)

From Kansas to Western Pennsylvania was a long, hard trip—almost 1200 miles. And, of course, heading east, we lost a couple of hours, which didn't help a bit. We left Kansas the morning of August 10, and had a meeting scheduled at Somerset, Pennsylvania the night of the 11th. On the way we had to sandwich in some very necessary errands—like finding a shoe repair shop to fix a broken heel on the only dress shoes I had with me! In order to meet our appointment, we drove on and on into the night; and when we finally decided we were too weary to go another inch, we just couldn't find a motel! Finally at 3:30 A. M. we found one, but it had only two rooms vacant, and we needed three. I nobly offered to sleep on the air mattress stretched out on one side of the station wagon. But since one room had a double bed and a single, it was decided that I should share that room with the Richardses. How Mary Richards laughed as I stumbled wearily into the room, kicked off my sandals, and climbed into bed, clothes and all! How tired can one get? Well, just that tired! We were there for only three or four hours anyway, I reasoned.

At 7:30 A. M. we were on our way again (it seemed to me that we had just gone to bed!), and arrived on the Somerset, Pennsylvania, campground at 7:30 P. M.—15 minutes before we were due on the platform! Again there was a scurry to find rooms in which to change, and a mad dash to get into the meeting. After the service, we had a little meeting especially for those who had responded to a call to give their hearts completely to God. As Pastor Richards was talking very solemnly to the group who had remained, in walked a very innocent-looking skunk! Yes, I said skunk! Everyone gasped—no one knew what to do. Mr. Skunk was treated with the utmost respect, and eventually someone lured him out. We had thought it rather unusual when, in Kansas, a little bitty mouse ran under Olive Braley's piano bench; but this topped Kansas!

Chapter Eighteen

After our duties at the Somerset camp meeting were fulfilled Saturday night, Mary and I felt the need of some exercise. The others—too exhausted after eleven hours of meetings, a radio interview, and personal contacts with people—refused our invitation to go for a hike. So we struck out alone, and ended up exploring a cemetery! Reading the names and epitaphs on the tombstones, we couldn't help wondering about the stories behind each person. A number of them were only in their twenties and thirties when they died. We wondered, too, if they had been ready to die. On one tombstone, I think it was dated 1812, we read a very thought-provoking inscription: "As you are, I was. As I am, you'll be. Prepare to follow me."

We turned homeward, but still had appointments at Cleveland and Dayton, Ohio; St. Elmo, Illinois, and East St. Louis, Illinois. In St. Louis, Missouri, we actually had a little "play time," the only whole afternoon we had on the entire trip that was our very own. And do you know how we chose to spend this precious time? We went to the fabulous St. Louis Zoo and saw the unforgettable elephant, lion, and monkey shows. At the monkey show, I turned around and saw Brad Braley laughing so hard at their antics that he had to wipe the tears from his eyes.

Next and last was Denver, Colorado, where we had two meetings in a large high school auditorium on August 19. The auditorium holds about 2500 or more, and the place was packed. At last came August 20, and our duties were over. We were all anxious to get home.

Yes, 12,867 more miles for the Master! I wonder, How long will it be until we take that thrilling trip through space with Christ when He comes to take home "His loved and His own"?

Wow! Can you imagine a trip like that: with ten stops for meetings, all in less than three weeks. We had five good-sized adults crammed together in a station wagon carrying all the clothing we would need for constant public appearances! You can get some idea of just how cramped our quarters were from the fact that I had taken only one pair of dress shoes with me.

Brad and Olive Braley were my traveling companions for nineteen summers! I didn't keep a record of how many miles we drove together each year, but all together it must have been enough to wear out two or three good cars. Brad would play the organ, and Olive would join in on the piano. They were very popular with audiences wherever we went. Olive was also a bit of an actress, and enjoyed doing dramatic readings and giving talks. They made a great team, and great teammates. When Brad passed away in 1992, I wrote a tribute to him in the *VOP News*, and described him this way:

> Dear, gentle, kind, thoughtful, willing, humble, loving—these are just a few of the adjectives that came into my mind when I was asked to pay tribute to a man with whom I traveled many thousands of miles for over 19 years as my accompanist and fellow musician. . . .
>
> You really get to know people when you travel with them and also spend many pressure-filled hours in a recording studio. I've seen Brad weary, sick, and under many different circumstances—some happy, some trying—and through it all his kindness, cheerfulness, and lovely disposition always surfaced. . . .
>
> Brad would go anywhere he was asked to go and play anything available, although sometimes he'd whisper in my ear that "the only remedy for this piano (or organ) is kerosene and a match."
>
> I recall one exception to his willingness. We were asked to help in the junior division at a camp meeting. The piano at the junior tent was horrendous. Brad made a noble attempt to play it, and I bravely tried to capture the children's attention with my songs. Understandably, the children began giggling at the weird sounds that came from the grossly out-of-tune piano that had many broken keys. (Oh, for some kerosene and a match!)

Chapter Eighteen

Brad stopped and looked up at me with a distressed "cocker spaniel" look. "Del, I'm sorry, I can't play this thing. It's hopeless!" By this time, the kids were cracked up, I was hysterical, and Brad's distress turned to giggles as he put his head down on the piano. We had a good time with the children, anyway, singing a cappella and sharing with them.

One thing I didn't mention in that article was that as kind and caring and hardworking as he was, Brad also had a little tendency toward being a hypochondriac. Every stomachache seemed to him like the onset of a major flu, and a little cough meant a cold was coming on. Once I decided to have a little fun with him, just to see what would happen. Traveling along in the station wagon, I was sitting in the back seat, when I suddenly faked a sneeze. "Oh, I hope I'm not coming down with a cold," I said.

"I hope not, too," Brad responded, and I could tell he was worried that he might catch it from me if I was. Amazingly, the next day he actually did have a cold! I felt so guilty. What a naughty thing to do!

One of Brad's best qualities was his concern for souls. When we traveled in the summer, we kept some of our suitcases and supplies in a luggage rack on top of the station wagon. Well, one hot, muggy day, I was driving on the freeway in Louisiana when the rack suddenly broke loose; suitcases, boxes of supplies, and the precious interest cards that people had signed at camp meetings went flying. There were clothes hanging from bushes, suitcases in the median, and interest cards everywhere. I'm not sure exactly how long we spent combing the median and both shoulders of that superhighway, but it seemed like hours. Brad was so concerned that we not lose one card signed by a person who wanted Bible studies or some other information, that we had to be sure we found every one of the cards that had scattered like the leaves of autumn.

I was able to go and visit Brad and Olive shortly before Brad died. They were living in a nursing home in Loma Linda, and Olive wasn't able to get up, but Brad came out to greet me. "How about playing a couple of oldies for me?" I asked. The room contained a small organ.

Brad was only too delighted to play "Sweet By and By" and "What a Friend We Have in Jesus."

"Beautiful. Sounds just like old times," I said, choking back the tears.

Brad got a wistful look in his eye and said, "Those were the golden years. Didn't we have a great time working at the good old VOP, Del!"

Well, we sure did. Trips like the 1961 itinerary were hectic, rushed, sometimes frustrating. But I wouldn't trade those years for anything. Fortunately, by the time I started traveling extensively for the VOP, most of the cars we used had air conditioning. But that wasn't the case in the beginning. This sort of touring had been going on every year since the middle 1940s. I've heard Bob Edwards, who joined the King's Heralds in 1947, tell about how they used to dread those long summer trips in the big, black 1938 Cadillac. He remembers stopping regularly in Needles, California, right on the Arizona border on Route 66. There was a little ice cream shop there, where they would all get milk shakes. Then the men would take their shirts off and rub themselves with ice to try to stay a little bit cool on their trip across the desert.

That would only last for a short while though. Soon they would be sweltering, and they had a whole summer of that kind of heat to look forward to. It's a wonder any of us survived and kept on doing it year after year. But we knew we had an important mission to fulfill, and we couldn't let a little inconvenience or discomfort stop us. After all, Jesus didn't let the smell of the stable, the slivers in the carpenter shop, or the nails in the cross stop Him from coming to earth to save us!

I summed up the way we looked at the "privilege" of travel in another article I wrote, reporting on our itinerary in 1959: " 'Do you like to travel?' you ask. We answer, Yes, we consider it a real privilege and joy to have a part in anything that God is using to change lives and to prepare people for a place in His soon-coming kingdom."

I really do consider myself to have been privileged to go so far and do so many things in the cause of the kingdom. In fact, some of the most interesting events of my entire life have occurred while I was on the road. More about that in the following chapters.

Chapter Nineteen

One of the first times that I remember going on a long trip instead of just doing weekend appointments or evangelistic series around southern California was in 1952, the year after I went to Europe with Leona Running. Maybe when I survived that trip, the managers at the VOP began to see me differently and decided they ought to take advantage of my apparent wanderlust by sending me on longer journeys. Anyhow, for whatever reason, the end of May that year found me attending the Blue Ridge Summer Camp near Ashville, North Carolina, with The Chief and the King's Heralds. After our time together there, the others went to Arkansas, but I headed for Orlando, Florida, where I spent a week singing in various meetings at a convocation there. Then I represented the VOP at a camp meeting in Tennessee for nine days. Later that month I joined Pastor Richards, his wife, Mabel, and the King's Heralds on a trip to Hawaii to attend the Pan Pacific Youth Congress there.

In retrospect those trips must have been my "shakedown cruise" because itineraries became a lot more complex a few years later.

One early trip I remember came in 1956, when Brad Braley and I were sent to several meetings in northern California. For years there has been a splendid camp meeting held at a place called Soquel in the San Francisco Bay Area. The thing I remember about Soquel is that one of the times I sang there years later, the music director for the meetings was a man with a doctorate in music, and he wasn't at all thrilled when the administration told him he had to invite me to sing. I guess he thought of me as just a simple gospel singer who wasn't up to his level. When I arrived on the campground, he looked at me like I was chopped liver. But there was nothing he could do, so he figured he'd just tough it out and hope it would be over soon.

The song I'd planned to sing at the opening meeting was "The Lord's Prayer" by Malotte. It goes up to a high D, even in the low arrangement I use, and I wasn't terribly confident that I'd be able to hit that note convincingly. I prayed about it, as I always do before I sing, asking the Lord to bless my efforts, and I was relieved when I managed to hit the note squarely. Afterward the music director came to me and said with a new look of respect, "I didn't know you could sing things like that."

With a smile I asked, "Doctor, did it take that to make you respect me?"

You meet so many people along the way when you travel, and most of them are wonderful. I suppose that story has stuck in my mind because it was the exception rather than the rule.

One of my best trips ever was the three weeks I spent traveling with a great group of musicians in 1967.

The late '60s were a time of great turmoil in our country. The Vietnam War sparked hostilities and protests back home, and, of course, the Civil Rights movement was still very much an issue as well. Inside conservative churches though, the conflict centered around other issues, including what type of music was appropriate for church, and especially for the youth. The Beatles had stormed across from England, bringing a whole new type of music with them. Meanwhile folk singers like Bob Dylan, Pete Seeger, and Joan Baez had begun to be active in the protest movements, causing many people to associate folk music with something negative.

Right in the midst of this troubled time, three Adventist boys from America, Bob Summerour, Jerry Hoyle, and Don Vollmer, went to England to study at Newbold College for a year. While they were there, they began playing, singing, and composing American folk music together. They became very popular in England, and when they returned to the U. S. the next year, their reputation began to spread.

But they had two strikes against them in many people's minds. They'd formed their group in England, where the Beatles came from, and they sang folk music, which associated them with the protest movements. So there was little chance they would find much acceptance within the musically and politically conservative Seventh-day Adventist Church. In some people's minds, just the fact that their main instruments were guitars, banjos, and a bass fiddle (strummed, not bowed) made them unfit company.

But Harold Richards didn't see it that way at all. Both he and I always had a special burden for reaching out to young people, speaking to them in ways that would attract them rather than driving them away. Harold heard these three young fellows, who called their group Wedgwood, play at a youth rally he attended, and he saw how the young people responded to them.

That planted an idea in his head. If the VOP was going to reach the younger generation, maybe we needed to broaden the spectrum of music we used.

It wasn't long before Harold had proposed that we invite Wedgwood to join Group B for our summer tour in 1967.

Believe me, there were some at the VOP who thought Harold had lost his mind, and others who argued vehemently against any change in the style of music we associated ourselves with. But Harold knew we needed to try new things if we were going to continue to have a positive influence in the world. In that, he took after his father, who had the courage to step out and use radio to broadcast the gospel at a time when many people thought that Christians shouldn't have anything to do with it.

When I heard Wedgwood's music, I was thrilled. Sure it was folk music. But it was music with a positive Christian message. I didn't see why it should be condemned just because of its style and the type of instruments it was played on. I've heard that Louis Armstrong once said, "All music is folk music. You ain't never heard a horse sing, have you?"

But all joking aside, I admired Harold for his decision and supported him in it. From June 8-25, 1967, Wedgwood joined Harold, the Braleys, and me on our camp-meeting itinerary to seven states. Later that summer, Harold traveled with Wedgwood to nine more states. Surprisingly, they were well accepted most places, but there were a couple of camp meetings where they were severely limited as to when and where they could perform.

The irony of it is that years later they returned to one of the camp meetings where they had encountered the most opposition and had been allowed to perform only in the youth tent. Thirty years later, when they returned, still singing the same songs, the leaders at the youth tent wouldn't have them—their music was passé. But the adult auditorium welcomed them with open arms!

I think it may have been from that state that the trio received one of their most touching testimonials. There was a young lady whose father heard Wedgwood was coming and strictly forbade his teenage daughter to attend. Somehow she sneaked out and listened to their music anyhow. A few weeks later they received a letter from her, telling how she had been so moved by their music and their positive, upbeat attitude toward Christianity that she had given her heart to the Lord during their concert. Never before had she seen anyone who made religion so real and meaningful to her.

I think that summer of '67 was one of the finest ever for the VOP traveling teams. It was a good experience to help us get in contact with a younger generation. A few years later, the Way Out materials we produced were another attempt to broaden our outreach and include everyone.

Considering the amount of controversy that arose from Harold's decision to take Wedgwood on tour, you can imagine the reaction I got when I suggested that maybe I ought to do a recording with them. I was about as popular as a skunk at a picnic with some of the people in our music department. But I believed it was the right thing to do, and I kept talking to different people around the office, asking What's wrong with that kind of music, anyhow? Finally I was given the go-ahead. I really enjoyed recording with Wedgwood, because it was totally different from anything I'd ever done before. I loved the gospel music I was known for, but felt it was time to include this style too. Like me, they didn't work with a musical score in front of them— just words. Bob Summerour was the inspiration behind a lot of the arrangements they did, but they all worked together. They just had a feel for the way to create the sound they wanted, and it flowed naturally from them.

In retrospect, I wish I would have had a little more experience singing with a folk sound. I think I could have done it better, but the album we produced, called *Joyful*, was one of my most popular ones. I really wish I'd had a chance to do another album with them, even though some people thought I'd gone off the deep end, and some shared their feelings with me in no uncertain terms. One musician I had worked with in the past even wrote to me and told me I ought to go out in the woods and study the life of Christ until I was reconverted. He figured that my taste in music indicated I had lost my contact with the Lord. I wrote back and told him that I kept *The Desire of Ages*, a book on the life of Christ, beside my bed and read it often, thank you very much! I don't think we should pass spiritual judgment on people over matters of personal taste.

I still defend my willingness to reach out to a new generation with their music—within reason, of course. Now that doesn't mean I don't think we need to draw the line somewhere. Just a few years ago I was invited to sing on one of our church's college campuses, at an outdoor concert. I was really surprised when I arrived there to discover that a rock band was sharing the stage with me. They would sing a few songs (if you can call it singing!), and then I would get up and sing. The contrast couldn't have been more dramatic. I couldn't imagine why they had invited someone like me to join that concert, and I have to say that I can't get into the kind of music where the instruments make so much noise that the singers have to scream to be heard at all, and it's almost impossible to understand what they are saying. Afterward a young man who was part of the rock group came up to me and asked, "What do you think of our music, Del?"

I was honest with him. I said, "If you can't understand the words, and the rhythm and the instruments cover up the message, what are you doing?"

His reply surprised me. "That's just exactly what I told our leader," he said. "Thank you. I think I'll be getting out of this group." I sensed that he just needed me to affirm him in a decision he had already made.

The matter of taste and choices in music is a touchy one. I think Christian music ought to have a clear, understandable message, and that the message should not be overpowered by the volume or rhythm, forcing the listener to strain to hear the words. Personally, I happen to admire Sandi Patty's vocal range and have enjoyed many of her songs through the years. But recently a young lady came up to me after I had sung at a church and told me she'd recently been to one of Sandi's concerts. After we talked for a moment about the beauty of Sandi's voice, the girl said, "I loved Sandi's concert, but I'm glad to have a chance to hear you again. It's good to get back to the simple things."

I smiled to myself and thought, *Not everyone can be a gourmet item. I'm happy to be one of the simple things if the Lord can use me!*

I've found it to be so true through the years that different musicians and styles appeal to different people, and we shouldn't try to force everyone into our mold. I remember a trip to Mexico when another woman musician—a soprano named Maurita Thornburgh—traveled with us. She has a gorgeous voice. Some people flocked to her. Others flocked to me. But we didn't have to be in competition. We were both pleased to be meeting the needs of those who loved our music.

Not long ago I received a phone call from a lady, complaining about my taste in music. She had seen me singing at one of The Voice of Prophecy Family Reunion concerts and had noticed that I had joined in clapping my hands with the rhythm in some of the songs. She wanted me to know how disappointed she was that I had fallen so low. I pointed out that the Bible doesn't condemn clapping; in fact in Psalm 47 it admonishes us to clap our hands. Then I went on to tell her that the greatest hope of my life is to see Jesus coming on the clouds of glory. When I see that, I'm not going to just stand there, silently smiling. I'm going to get really excited! Clapping my hands won't be enough—I think I'll be turning cartwheels!

I'm not sure I persuaded her that a little joyfulness in our music is appropriate, but I hope so. I really think music was given to us to help cheer us up when we're down, and to give us courage when life is difficult. At least it has often served that purpose in my life, and many people have written to me and told me how music has helped them as well. One story that particularly stands out in my life came from a woman whose husband was a psychiatrist. She was very depressed, even suicidal, and, of course, her husband had done everything he could to help her and motivate her, give her a reason to live. One night she turned on our broadcast and heard me sing "The Night Watch"—a song that has gotten terrific response through the years. After she heard the song, she wrote to us and got the record that had the song on it. When she wrote to me later, she said that it had totally turned her life around. That one simple song, sung by one simple singer, accomplished more than all the things her husband and his colleagues had tried to do for her. She said it probably saved her life.

Music touches feelings that words cannot, and so we must be careful in how we use it and how we perform it. Somewhere I picked up this little statement, and I'm not sure where it came from, but it hits the nail right on the head, as far as I'm concerned, about how music should be used: "Unless our music is an unfolding of the meaning of the Scriptures, we are only performers and what we are doing is not a ministry and people will not be truly helped and blessed by just a performance. Singers who resist the temptation to be diluted with too much of their own expertise and personality will be truly effective in glorifying God and moving the hearts of people heavenward. No one can at the same time call attention to himself and to Christ. If people go away from our preaching or singing saying, 'My what a wonderful preacher (or singer)' or 'What a fantastic voice' and that's all they're saying, we have failed. Success is when they are overwhelmed by the message of the song or sermon and go away saying, 'My, what a great God we have!' "

When I worked with Wedgwood, I sensed that they were not just performers. They had a message that would touch many hearts, and I've always been happy that I had the chance to sing with them.

The year after we toured with Wedgwood proved to be one of our busiest travel seasons ever, and one of the most fruitful. It carried us across the United States and Canada, and then down to South America. But I'd better save that for the next chapter.

Chapter Twenty

From 1961 until 1967, Group B included Harold Richards, the Braleys, and myself. We logged tens of thousands of miles crisscrossing North America together, visiting thirty-seven states from Maine to California and Washington to Florida, plus four Canadian provinces. During the second half of the summer of '67, Harold and Wedgwood, along with Gordon and Phyllis Henderson went together. I finished out the summer traveling with the Braley's once again, but with Pastor J. J. Aitken occupying the other seat in the station wagon and doing the preaching at meetings we attended.

In the spring of 1968, Harold conducted evangelistic meetings in Portland, Oregon, and Saskatoon, Saskatchewan, and I was able to join him for each of those series. We liked to hold meetings like that in places where the broadcast had been getting a lot of attention. Listeners would come to hear us, and many took their stand as Christians as a result.

During the summer, I traveled with the Braleys and two different speakers to camp meetings in half a dozen states and three Canadian provinces. But all of this was just leading up to the real major trip of the year—a trip that would take The Chief, Brad Braley, and me to hold meetings in seven South American countries in seven weeks.

Chapter Twenty

We began in Brazil because *The Voice of Prophecy* radio program there was celebrating its silver anniversary.

During World War II, shortly after the U. S. broadcast went nationwide on the Mutual network, Pastor Roberto Rabello from Brazil came to visit The Chief in Glendale. One thing I'd like you to know about the founder of the VOP is that he never let his worldwide fame go to his head, never strove to advance himself, never considered anyone to be competition. As long as someone wanted to proclaim the gospel, The Chief was on their side, and would help him or her any way he could. Whenever he was in the office, there seemed to be a constant stream of young pastors coming to visit and get advice, and he was always very gracious, probably taking more time than he could really afford to talk with them.

So, when Pastor Rabello told The Chief that he admired what he was doing and wanted to emulate it in his own country, the full resources of the VOP were put to use to help make it happen. It wasn't long before the King's Heralds were recording songs in Portuguese for use on the broadcast, and when I began to sing for the ministry, I was soon invited to try my hand at that language as well.

By the end of 1943, The Voice of Prophecy was being broadcast in Portuguese to the Brazilian people, with Pastor Rabello as the speaker. By the silver anniversary date in 1968, we were being heard on more than 300 stations all over the country. Because of this, and because of the enthusiasm of the lay church members for inviting friends to come with them, we were met by large crowds wherever we went. The Brazilian people were so open and accepting of us and seemed to really love our music, and we quickly learned to love them as well. As it turned out, this was to be only the first of five trips to Brazil for me, the last one coming in 1993 for the golden anniversary celebration.

The only problem I encountered while traveling there was one that I've had in many countries where languages other than English are spoken. With the help of some excellent coaches and the blessing of the Holy Spirit, I've had the privilege of recording songs in fifteen different languages. That was no easy task, and many times I just couldn't seem to get a pronunciation right, but then we would bow our heads and ask the Lord for a special blessing, and somehow the sounds would come out just right.

So, when I would sing in Brazil, of course I would use songs I'd already learned in their language. The listening crowds would hear me singing in perfect Portuguese and naturally assume that I spoke their language. You can imagine what a Tower of Babel it was at the end of the service when dozens of people would crowd around, all speaking rapidly in Portuguese, assuming I was understanding everything they said. In reality, I was understanding absolutely nothing. My conversation was limited to saying Thank you and a few other phrases.

The same sort of thing happened in the Spanish-speaking countries we visited next. The speaker for *La Voz de la Esperanza (The Voice of Hope)* at that time was Pastor Braulio Pérez, who had started broadcasting in Spanish in 1942 under the umbrella of the VOP.

It seems like it was only a few days after I arrived at the VOP that I was sitting at my desk busily typing a letter, when I became aware of someone standing in the doorway of my office, waiting for me to look up. When I invited him in, he introduced himself and asked me whether I would consider singing for the Spanish broadcast.

"Oh, no, Pastor Pérez," I said. "Thank you for asking me, but I don't know a thing about singing in Spanish or pronouncing it. I'd be afraid to even try—I don't think I could do an acceptable job." This was no false modesty on my part. Remember, I hadn't felt confident enough to come to the VOP and sing in English when I was first invited. Now, to think of singing in a language I knew nothing about? Not a chance.

But Pastor Pérez was not to be put off so easily. When I said I didn't think I could do an acceptable job, he just smiled and said, "You let me be the judge of that. Are you willing to at least try? I'll help you."

How could I turn down a request like that? Soon I was in the studio, attempting to get the pronunciation of words I'd never seen before in my life just so. "Sharper *l*'s please," Pastor Pérez would say, or "Roll those *r*'s." Sometimes he'd tease me. "No, we can't use that. You sound like a gringo!"

Chapter Twenty

Many times I marveled at his patience, along with his tenacity, when we were striving to polish and produce a song that would sound right to Spanish-speaking people. There were times when I'd get so frustrated I just wanted to crawl away into a corner and have a good cry, but sensing my distress, he would come up with some clever witticism that would make me laugh instead, and we'd keep on trying until I got it right.

How I wished for the gift of tongues during those sessions. But I remember only one time in my whole life when I seemed to have that gift. It happened in Mexico in 1973. I was traveling with Pastor Pérez, and he took me to the home of the Johnny Carson of Mexico, whose name was George Saldaña. The King's Heralds and I had been invited to sing on his program *Sabado con Saldaña* a number of times. While we were at his home, Mr. Saldaña asked me to sing for him. Pastor Pérez suggested I sing "Lonely Voices," but I hadn't memorized it in Spanish. "That's OK," he said. "Just sing it for him in English."

So that's what I did. Imagine my amazement sometime later when Pastor Pérez told me that Mr. Saldaña had complimented me not only on my voice, but on my Spanish pronunciation. Apparently he had heard the song in Spanish! If only it were always that easy to sing in a foreign language! While I'm on the topic of Spanish speakers, I should tell you that after Pastor Pérez turned over the torch to his successor, Milton Peverini, I had the privilege of traveling many places with Pastor Peverini in the Spanish-speaking world. Then Frank Gonzales took over, and I have traveled some with him as well. I marvel at how God finds just the right people to carry on His work. I have the highest respect for all three of these godly gentlemen.

Getting back to our 1968 trip to South America, we left Brazil after several hectic days of travel and landed next in Uruguay. What a delight it was to be met at the airport by my old friend Pastor Pérez. What adventures we had in the next few weeks as we traveled together, singing and preaching to packed houses in large stadiums and auditoriums all over South America. Although I couldn't understand much of what he was saying when he spoke in Spanish, I could tell by the intensity with which people gazed at him that he was making every word count.

One of the things I'll always remember about that trip was the time I spent with my special friend Charlie. No, I didn't have a passionate Latin romance south of the border. My friend was a marmoset—a tiny South American monkey. I met him in Bolivia, when we went to the home of Pastor and Mrs. Scully. They had a fifteen-year-old daughter named Margaret, and Charlie was her pet—very devoted to her. He didn't like strangers at all, they told me.

But apparently I was no stranger to him, because the minute I walked in the door, our eyes met, and it was love at first sight. Charlie was sitting on Margaret's shoulders one moment, and an instant later he had jumped over onto mine. And from that time on, it was virtually impossible to pry him loose.

There was even a time when I was scheduled to give a live concert on the radio. As we went into the station building, Charlie began clinging to me, hanging around my neck even tighter than before, peering around with his big, brown eyes. When someone tried to take him away, he put up such a fuss that I said, "Oh, just leave him. He'll be OK."

And OK he was. All through the concert, he just hung on my neck. There was a studio audience at the radio station, and I've often wondered what the people who were watching thought. Maybe they just thought I had a fur stole around my neck. But every time I'd hit a particularly high note, Charlie would quiver.

Another time we were traveling from one city to another, and Charlie was in the car with us. I tried to coax him onto my lap, but he wouldn't come. In fact, he seemed a little disturbed—wouldn't settle down anywhere. Then someone opened a window, and you'll never guess what Charlie did. He backed up to the window and relieved himself! The Chief was with us, watching all this happen, and he burst out laughing. I often saw him laugh. He had a great sense of humor and would even pull jokes on people sometimes to lighten up the moment. But I had never seen him laugh that hard. When he finally regained his composure enough to speak, he said, "Del, Charlie was too much of a gentleman to do that in your lap!" We laughed about that experience many times after that.

We hardly had a moment's rest that whole seven weeks of travel. On that trip and subsequent trips to South America, I learned that our ministers there are extremely hard workers. Many of them travel regularly between a dozen or more churches, and Pastor Pérez was certainly no slacker either. After two or three strenuous itineraries down there, I started calling "uncle." When the next invitation to tour around South America would come, I'd ask to see the schedule before accepting. That way I could assure that we'd at least get a little rest and time to recuperate instead of driving ourselves so hard that we ended up sick.

We enjoyed associating with the enthusiastic crowds in Brazil, Uruguay, Argentina, Chile, Ecuador, Peru, and Bolivia. And when we got back to the U. S., we were especially pleased to learn that the national legislature of Brazil had entered into the record of their session a special congratulatory message for our Brazilian broadcast. What a thrill it was to read the translation of this message, which said, "The House, so concerned about people's problems, could not neglect to say a few words of gratitude and appreciation on the Silver Jubilee of the best evangelistic radio program ever broadcast in Brazil. It has accomplished through Bible messages and songs, the largest sowing of Christian faith that Brazilian radio has ever had."

But as great and important as the events in South America were, there was something happening back home about this time that gave me an even greater thrill.

Chapter Twenty-One

My mother became a Seventh-day Adventist at age eighteen after attending a series of evangelistic meetings. But not much of her family followed her example. I shared the story of the preacher's "premadies" in chapter six. As a direct result of that bad experience, my mothers' sisters had very little to do with her church for the rest of their lives—a great tragedy I believe, because the Church has a wonderful message. It's too bad that one particular preacher turned his back on the sinless Christ in his sermon and focused instead on what he considered the sins of my aunts.

Because Mother was so busy and worked so hard when Stan and I were young, we didn't always get to church on a regular basis, and as a result both of us kind of turned our back on religion for a time. So I've never ceased to marvel at the series of miracles that happened to lead me to associate first with The Quiet Hour, and then with the VOP. And I've never ceased to be thankful to Bob Thompson for insisting that I go to The Quiet Hour and to Pastor Tucker for making Jesus and heaven so real and attractive and for helping me see that religion wasn't just about giving up things that I wanted.

But while all this was happening, Stan was nowhere around. In 1941 he had gone to work at the General Cable Company in Oakland and was often assigned to help set up manufacturing plants in other cities. Meanwhile he was taking engineering classes by correspondence. During the war, he became supervisor of the navy department at General Cable and also met a beautiful blue-eyed blonde named Claire Nelson. He and Claire were married on April 6, 1943; two weeks later Stan entered the army and soon shipped out to England.

Stan came back from the war unscathed (although he once had a bullet go right through his helmet) and went back to work at General Cable. But religion just wasn't important to him. I wanted so badly to share my love for Christ with him, but there seemed to be a wall separating us that just wouldn't let us get to that subject. So I decided the best thing to do was just to live my faith whenever I visited and hope that would be an adequate witness.

But sometime in the 1960s, I had a dream so vivid that it woke me up. It was such a beautiful dream at first, but it turned into a nightmare. In the opening scene I was outside looking up at the sky, when I suddenly realized Jesus was coming in the clouds of glory. I was so excited! I couldn't believe my eyes and ears. "This is it!" I shouted ecstatically. Angels were coming down from the clouds, gathering up the saved, and taking them up to be with Jesus for all eternity. Then, suddenly, it was as if a curtain came down over the scene. I couldn't see Jesus anymore. And then, projected on that curtain was my brother's face. He was looking at me sternly, disgusted, as I'd often seen him do when we were younger. He said just five words to me: "Why didn't you warn me?"

I was so startled by his question that I awoke. At first it seemed to me like Jesus had really come and that I had been left behind, but then I realized it was just a dream. It made a deep impression on me, and I began to think maybe I should do something more to win Stan back to Christ.

The next night I had the exact same dream. And the next night too. It came three nights in a row! And by then I was sure that the next time I saw Stan, things were going to be different.

A few weeks later I went up to Oakland to visit Stan and Claire and their sons Joel and Dennis, and as soon as I got a chance, I pulled Stan aside and told him all about my dream. "Jesus is coming back again—soon—Stan," I said. "And I want you to be ready! You're never going to look at me and say, 'Why didn't you warn me?' "

I don't know how much of an impression that first appeal made. Stan was very involved in his work. He was a top executive for General Cable by then, and church and religion just didn't get high priority with him. But I continued to visit occasionally and always talked to him about spiritual things and making a commitment to Jesus. I can remember one night when we talked about these things until three o'clock in the morning.

Conviction gradually began to take hold of Stan, but he just didn't figure he could take a stand. "What about my family?" he said. "I haven't given them a lick of spiritual training. If I all of a sudden get religious on them, they're not going to want me around anymore."

Well, that was an excuse God knew how to deal with. During my visits with Stan's family I had become very close to Claire, and one time I shared one of my favorite books with her, *Drama of the Ages* by W. H. Branson. The book reviews all the history of the Bible and the modern world and shows how God has been working behind the scenes in all of it. Using prophecies and other Scripture texts, it points to the soon coming of Jesus.

The book made a deep impression on Claire, and she began to study the Bible. Finally there came the day when she made a commitment and was baptized. I was there and sang at the church service. Then I went to Stan and said, "Now what's your excuse, brother?"

He could no longer hide behind the excuse of family. But what really troubled him was that he was so devoted to his work at General Cable that he feared that "getting religion" would interfere with his job and he wouldn't be able to carry on. But conviction continued to wear away at his peace until on May 25, 1968, just before I had to leave on my first summer itinerary, Stan was baptized and joined the Church. I was there and sang at the service.

He soon found out that this had been his best decision ever. It didn't interfere with his work—he was still highly valued by his company—so much so that when he retired fifteen years later, they asked him to continue to serve as a consultant and sent him on trips all over the world to represent the company.

So, you can see what I meant when I said that more important things—to me anyhow—were happening back home than in South America in 1968.

With Stan and Claire safely entrusting their eternal life to their Savior, I began to focus more of my attention on their sons, Joel and Dennis. But before I tell you about them, let me turn to something else that had happened just a few years earlier.

I told you already that my mother left my father before I was even born. They were officially divorced before my second birthday, and I have little memory of ever having seen him as a child. He never wrote to his children or sent us presents for our birthdays or Christmas. I resented that. Mother wasn't the type to tell stories to turn Stan and me against our father, but other members of the family had said negative things about him. Just the fact that I never heard from him or saw him led me to have very harsh feelings toward him.

After I was converted, I tried to change my attitude—I even prayed for him from time to time, and my attitude did change a bit, but still I couldn't bring myself to love him. Then, one day, sometime in the late '50s, I believe, a letter came to the VOP from Andrew Delker. He said that he had heard a woman named Del Delker singing on the radio, and he just wondered if that could by any chance be his daughter.

I wrote back to him—several times, in fact. By that I mean, I had to tear the letter up the first three times I wrote because I was afraid it was going to catch fire in the typewriter! The depths of my feelings of abandonment and resentment surprised me.

Finally, after a few days, my spirit softened, and I began to think of my father as another candidate for the kingdom that I should minister to instead of chastising, and I wrote another letter that I could feel good about mailing. I think the only barb I put in it was a sentence that said something like, Yes, I'd heard that a lady named Martha and a man named Andrew were responsible for my coming into the world.

I didn't have a lot of contact with him after that, but in the early '60s I heard that he was suffering with multiple sclerosis—a severely debilitating disease—and I felt sorry for him. He had actually begun to have symptoms in 1940, and by this time he wasn't able to do much at all. I think it was in 1961 or 1963 when I was in South Dakota on a VOP trip, one of my mother's brothers asked if I wanted to visit my father. I said Yes, and he took me to see him.

By that time my father was completely crippled. All he could do was lie in bed and look up at me. And all I felt for him then was pity, that this man who had once been so strong was now confined to a bed, destined for an early death.

I couldn't hate him anymore. But it wasn't until many years later, as I got to know and love my half-brother Harry and my half-sister Laverne, his two children by his second marriage, that I was able to begin to think positively about him. While preparing to write this book, I contacted Laverne and learned that my father had behaved very differently toward his second family. He had been a good, caring father. And she even told me that later in life he desperately wanted to meet Stan and me. He had saved up money three different times and traveled to California in search of us, but had never been able to locate us.

That made me feel differently about him, and today I hope and pray that in the kingdom of heaven I'll be able to spend time with the father I never had here on earth. He passed to his rest in 1964, with the Lord's Prayer on his lips.

Multiple sclerosis is not a hereditary disease, but the tendency toward it seems to run in families. None of my father's children suffered from it, but Stan's son Joel began to suffer the symptoms when he was still quite young. Joel had always been a special missionary project of mine. Scholarly and detached, he wasn't terribly impressed when his parents began attending church. That sort of thing wasn't for him. But as his symptoms grew more noticeable, and he came to realize his own frailty, something began to change in his heart. What really amazes me is that for some reason he decided to attend church up in Fresno one day—long before he had given any indication of interest in religion. The pastor at that time was Joe Melashenko, father of the current VOP Director/Speaker Lonnie Melashenko. Joe is a warm, outgoing true gentleman of Ukrainian background, and he just loves to give people big bear hugs. Joel normally wouldn't respond to that kind of thing, but somehow Joe's friendliness got through to him, and he began studying the Bible and was baptized sometime later.

Being the scholar that he was, Joel soon headed for Loma Linda University, where he received a doctorate in public health. But his disease continued to progress, and soon he was confined to a wheel-chair, then to bed. It broke Claire's heart to see her precious son suffering so. It hurt me deeply too, because I had always had a special love for both of Stan's sons. One day as Claire and I were visiting Joel, Claire broke down and said, "I just can't take this!"

Joel could barely speak at the time, but he looked up at her and said, "Mother, you'd better take it. If I hadn't gotten sick, I probably would never have become a Christian."

It didn't make it any easier to watch him slowly fade away. But it did give us hope that one day soon we'll see him again, and he and I can take a run together and maybe do a few cartwheels! Joel was only forty-one when he died.

Joel's brother Dennis didn't have multiple sclerosis, but he had serious problems with alcohol. How I prayed and prayed for him. He would get a little resolve and try to change his ways—he went through detoxification programs several times. But he always seemed to fall off the wagon again. It was hard to watch him go downhill. Just when things would start looking up, he'd be in trouble again. I began to think he was a hopeless case. Then, finally, on July 18, 1989, he realized he couldn't do it on his own and turned his life over to the Lord and was baptized. I'm proud to say that he has been sober for many years now and is an active member of a church up in Porterville. He and his wife, Irene, are very dear to me and go out of their way to let me know that they will always be in my corner. Denny comes to see me now with a Bible or a book like *The Desire of Ages* tucked under his arm.

As the busy year 1968 drew to a close, I began to realize that I was going to have to deal with a medical problem of my own before long.

Chapter Twenty-Two

My favorite recreational activity in the whole world is water skiing. I used to love to go down to the Salton Sea with a group of friends. We'd take turns skiing behind a boat owned by my mom's cousin, Dr. Enid Merkel. I loved to ski with his daughter Cindi and could easily pass a day doing that. But after I turned forty, I began to notice severe pains in my right hip after a day on the water. It didn't concern me at first; I figured it was just part of growing older. But it kept getting worse and worse, until I realized I had to give up water skiing. Finally I went to the doctor, and he told me that the hip had a serious problem.

I've often joked that my mother was a very pretty lady and she also had bone problems. She gave me the bone problems and kept her looks!

Actually the problem was not so much with the bones, but with the cartilage in the joint—or the lack thereof. Apparently something was wearing away the cartilage that's supposed to act as a cushion in the joint, and the doctor said that if things didn't improve, I'd soon have bone rubbing directly on bone. He suggested a surgery designed to correct a misalignment of my leg to prevent further excessive wear and tear on the cartilage.

As a child I was always quite athletic and loose-jointed. I can remember being able to bend over backward and touch the floor with my hands. The doctor said that people who are born that way sometimes have this type of problem with their joints later in life, but he was pretty sure he could get me all straightened out. (Later, I learned that I probably have an inherited disorder called Ehlers-Danlos Syndrome, which means that my collagen—the protein that's supposed to hold you together—is somehow defective.)

I didn't like the thought of surgery, but I did like the idea that he could do something that might ease the pain that was becoming constant by now, so I submitted to it in early 1969. The April issue of VOP News carried a picture of me in my hospital room, being visited by the King's Heralds, who had come by to cheer me up and sing for me.

I thought of this surgery as kind of preventive maintenance to keep me from having future problems.

Yeah, right!

Over the next thirty years I had to have five more surgeries on that same hip—one in 1971 and another in 1972. Finally in 1996 I had to have a complete hip replacement. But the artificial hip kept popping out. Over the next six months, my life became a series of accidents. I always had to be very careful, but as careful as I was, the joint would sometimes pop out and leave me helpless on the floor. Then in November it came out, and no one could get it back in. I had to be rushed to the hospital in an ambulance. So the doctor put a new joint in—a second major surgery within a seven-month period. That joint didn't prove to be any better. For the next three years I continued living in fear of my hip coming out of joint at inconvenient moments. All together I remember twenty times where my replacement hip popped out.

I kept a list of all the incidents, if you're interested! I'll give you just a sampling—so you can get a little bit of a feel for what I went through. The first replacement joint dislocated on July 2 and 21, again on August 20, and then finally on October 30; even the doctor couldn't get it to go back into joint. That's when he sent me to St. John's Hospital in Santa Monica, where specialist Dr. John Moreland put in a new total hip.

The new hip dislocated within two weeks—while I was still in the hospital. On January 23, 1997, I fell and broke my wrist when the hip popped out. After that, I was tired of calling an ambulance each time, and some of my neighbors and friends began to be pressed into service. Both Lonnie and Jeannie Melashenko have had the "privilege" of helping me, as has Phil Draper, and several of my neighbors. In 1998 I was scheduled to sing at a VOP Vision Builders meeting, when the hip came out in my hotel room. Phil, Lonnie, and Lonnie's brother Joedy all helped me that time, and I was on the stage singing a half hour later. But then five days later, the hip popped out while I was shopping in a supermarket. A total stranger had to help me. One time the hip dislocated while I was alone in a guestroom in Michigan at 2:00 A.M. I had to put it back all by myself that time.

As you can imagine, such a situation is extremely stressful, especially to a person who has to walk out on stage and sing without falling down!

Finally in 1999 Dr. Moreland told me about a newly-developed replacement hip called the constrained liner. After my twentieth incident, I consented to one more replacement, hoping it would be my last. I'm thankful to report that this new hip has solved my problem, and I'm now able to walk with confidence, not having to worry about suddenly landing on the ground in a humiliated heap. Incidentally, on one of my office visits, I learned from Dr. Moreland's receptionist that he's one of the most highly respected orthopedic surgeons in the world. He's operated on many movie stars, including Elizabeth Taylor.

Each of the surgeries was an extremely painful affair. In addition to the hip surgeries, I've had two left-knee surgeries. I had a total replacement of my left knee just a couple of years ago. That was the most painful of all the operations. I wouldn't wish this kind of trouble on anyone, but maybe there's been a bit of a purpose in it all. I notice as I travel that many people have heard about my multiple surgeries, and they like to come up and talk with me about them and share some of their own painful experiences. I believe the pain I've suffered has helped me be better able to minister to many of these people.

And another thing. I've told people if they want to find me when Jesus comes back to take us to heaven, just look for the lady with all

Chapter Twenty-Two

the flying body parts. That'll be me, because I know Jesus plans to replace all my aching joints with new ones with a lifetime warranty. Eternal lifetime, that is!

My hip is much better and more reliable now, but I haven't been water skiing lately. Actually, I've put in my order for a boat and water skis in heaven. That's a joke, of course, because we don't know just what heaven will be like, but if there's such a thing as water skiing there, you can look for me behind the fastest boat on the lake!

By June of 1969, I was well enough recovered to go traveling with the Braleys again, through Kansas, Texas, Nebraska, Idaho, and Washington, and later through several states in the east. In the '70s we started traveling a bit more by air from place to place instead of taking the long driving tours we had done for so many years. I can remember one itinerary when I traveled with VOP evangelist Fordyce Detamore. What a powerhouse that man was—he had more energy than a barrel of monkeys. He also enjoyed a good joke, and when my luggage got lost on one flight and I ended up wearing the same polka-dot dress to each meeting for the next two weeks, he teased me. "Del, I really love that dress," he said. "I've memorized every polka dot on it!" Maybe it was Fordyce who first shared this cute poem with me:

Two elephants, Harry and Faye
Couldn't kiss with their trunks in the way
So they boarded a plane
Now they're kissing in Maine
'Cause their trunks got sent to L. A.

I've chuckled many times over that poem, because travel by air can be really challenging. But I guess it's not as hard as what we used to do on those long road trips.

Fordyce was a hard worker who was known for spending many hours visiting interests during his evangelistic meetings. He'd be out early in the morning, and would even go visiting late at night after he had preached. He was also quite competitive, and the thing he liked to compete with me on was holding my breath. Whenever we'd stop at a motel with a pool, if we had time to go swimming, he'd challenge me—who can stay under the water longest! We were both pretty good, but since he was older than I was, I started worrying that he was going to pass out under the water sometime and drown. I never told him, but there were times when I would come up for air before I had to. I didn't want to be responsible for his untimely death.

The people I traveled the most with were Brad and Olive Braley. They were my constant companions in evangelism and visits to camp meetings and college campuses. Finally in 1972 Brad decided it was time to start thinking about retirement, and we began to audition new pianists for our music group. One of the things I liked to do was hand a potential accompanist one of my most difficult pieces like "Hallelujah, Home at Last!" and see how he or she could do at sight reading it. Wayne Hooper told me that if someone could sight-read that song without many mistakes the first time through, they could play almost anything.

After a careful auditioning process, a young African-American man who had just earned his master's degree in organ performance on a full scholarship at the University of Michigan was selected to join our team. Calvin Taylor began accompanying me part time in 1972, and became the full-time accompanist when Brad Braley retired in 1973. In March that year, Calvin accompanied Harold Richards and me on an extended evangelism itinerary that took us to Jamaica, the Bahamas, and Grand Cayman Island. Calvin was warmly received by the crowds there, but I have to tell you that he didn't meet as happy a reception on some of our itineraries. In fact, a pastor from one southern state called me up to invite me to come and give a concert in his church. "You have to understand," he explained. "This invitation is for you, Miss Delker. But we can't have your accompanist come this time. I think you understand, don't you?"

Yes, I understood what he meant. But I didn't understand his attitude. And I wouldn't accept it. I told him that Calvin and I were a team, and if Calvin wasn't welcome, well, neither was I, and I wouldn't be coming.

"Well, I'll have to take it back to my committee," the administrator said.

Chapter Twenty-Two

"You can take it to as many committees as you want," I said. "But I won't be coming without Calvin." I felt very strongly about that. How could people call themselves Christians and still discriminate against a man simply because of his skin color? It just wasn't right!

A few days later the man called back and said that both Calvin and I would be welcome at his church.

I never said anything to Calvin about my conversation, but somehow he must have sensed that he wasn't exactly welcome at this particular meeting. So the first time I was to sing, he asked if he could say a few words to the audience. I invited him to do so, and he stood up and sauntered across the platform. He came over to the microphone and bent down to speak right into it. "Hi, y'all," he said. "My name's Calvin Taylor, and I like watermelon."

That brought the house down, and the people seemed to go out of their way after that to make sure Calvin felt welcomed. I hope my taking a stand on the race issue had some lasting impact on people there.

Imagine—here was a brilliant musician who anyone should be proud of, but so-called Christian people didn't want him to come to their church because of his color! I couldn't understand it then, and I still can't. Actually, this was the only time this happened while Calvin worked with us. He was appreciated everywhere we went. After he left us he went on to earn a doctoral degree.

Calvin traveled with me for three years, all over the U. S. and Canada and on my second trip to Brazil in 1974. That was such an exciting and interesting trip. The Brazilian Voice of Prophecy Bible school was planning large graduations all over the country, and Pastor Rabello, the speaker, contacted me. "Del, you've been a soloist on our broadcast for twenty-five years now," he reminded me. "It was back in 1949 that I first started coaching you to sing in Portuguese, and the people here still love to hear you sing. Would it be possible for you to come and attend some of the graduations?"

Remembering how warmly I had been received in Brazil six years earlier, I just couldn't turn down the request. As plans for the itinerary developed, I learned that I'd not only be singing in Portuguese, but in German, Japanese, Spanish, and English as well. "Do you think you can manage all those languages?" I asked Calvin.

He just smiled. "Hey, I'll play in whatever language you like!" he said. I guess I've always had a little envy of musicians who play an instrument instead of sing—it's so much easier to translate their music into other languages!

When we got to Brazil, we launched right into visiting churches where Bible School graduations were being held, and it wasn't long before my voice started feeling the strain of travel and overuse. Within a few days I had laryngitis so bad that I could hardly speak above a whisper. Donna, one of my friends said to me, "Surely you're not going to try to sing sounding like that!"

"I have to sing," I responded. "I came a long way to sing for these people, and I'm going to put my feet in the Jordan River. The Lord will just have to help me to do the impossible!"

Somehow, whenever I stood up to sing, the voice that hadn't been there two minutes before would come back, and I was able to get through the song. I've seen this miracle occur over and over again during my years of ministry. In fact, it seems like my whole life has been full of miracles, with God providing just what I needed, when I needed it, as I dedicated my talents to His work.

I think it was on this trip to Brazil that one of my most embarrassing moments came. I'd been invited to sing for a television program in São Paulo, and when we arrived at the station, I was told to go right into the recording studio because they were almost ready for me. (I have to tell you that on this trip I traveled quite a bit with another of Brazil's great evangelists, but this man had a habit of getting us to appointments "just in time" or not quite on time. He knew it frustrated me when he would arrive late to take me somewhere, so he'd always bring me a box of chocolate bonbons to try to cheer me up. I think I left Brazil with several pounds of bonbons in my luggage!)

I rushed into the studio and the director gave the signal. It was one of the few times I sang along with a record (lip-synched), and wouldn't you know it, some klutz bumped the turntable half way through the song and the needle skipped. I had been told it was to be a taping session, not live. I thought well, that's OK, we can just stop and start over again, but they kept the record playing. I figured I knew how to make them stop, so I started cutting up, making all sorts of awful faces so they would have to stop. Then someone told me I was on the air—it was a live broadcast! I've never been so embarrassed in my life! I have no idea how many thousands of people were watching as I made a fool of myself. When I returned to the home where I had been staying, my hosts got call after call from friends who had been watching the telecast. "What was wrong with Del?" they all asked.

One of the highlights of our trip was a visit to Iguacu Falls on the border between Brazil and Argentina. I've been told that when Eleanor Roosevelt saw these huge falls she said, "Poor Niagra! Iguacu makes it look like the kitchen sink by comparison." The river is two-and-a-half miles wide at the falls, and the water drops 210 feet! We visited the falls on one of our rare days off while traveling, but even while we were there, a local pastor recognized us and told us he was holding evangelistic meetings in a tent nearby. Would it be possible for me to come and sing? he asked.

How could I turn down a request like that, so one more stop was added to our itinerary. At the end I enumerated what I had been able to do during the twenty-six day trip: I attended forty-two meetings in fourteen cities and sang a total of two hundred fifty-six songs in five languages. We hated to leave the friendly people of Brazil. They had presented us with so many flowers at every stop that we could easily have opened a florist shop before it was all over. But when the final day of the itinerary came, we had to admit we were ready for a vacation from traveling!

Calvin also went to the Philippines with me in 1976. We were traveling with Fordyce Detamore once again, and Calvin was the organist for a four-week evangelistic series in Manila. I sang every night at the meetings, including a few songs in Tagalog and Illocano, and on the weekends we toured around, visiting a different church each week. Then, after the meetings were over, we provided concerts at several locations in other parts of the country.

I'm not sure if all the traveling finally got to him, or whether he just sensed it was time to do something different, but in 1977 Calvin decided to devote himself full time to giving concerts. Once again, we found ourselves auditioning musicians. That's when I met Jim Teel. Only twenty-five years old, he'd majored in religion in college, but had taken as many music electives as he could. Because of his skill as a keyboard artist, composer, and arranger, he was able to win admission to a graduate music program at Arizona State University, where he earned a master's degree in music theory and composition.

All that was impressive enough. But when he sat down and played "Hallelujah, Home at Last" straight through with only a couple of mistakes the first time and then played it perfectly on his second attempt, both Wayne Hooper and I were sold! It wasn't just Jim's musicianship that made him a great addition to the team. He's also a very dedicated Christian with a positive, upbeat attitude toward life as a whole. Jim and I traveled all over the country together for the next five years with both H.M.S. Richards, Sr. and Jr., and sometimes just the two of us would go on a concert tour. We worked up a repertoire of around 200 songs together—we were a great team, I think. He was a fun person to travel with and could be a tease.

Imagine! He was only twenty-five years old when we started traveling together—the same year that I celebrated my thirtieth year of service with the VOP.

That was also the year I received one of my most treasured possessions. Everyone who ever heard one of the VOP broadcasts when The Chief was the speaker knows that he was a poet. He usually closed the program with a poem written just for the occasion. I never dreamed I'd have the honor of having a poem written just for me, but here's what he gave me on my thirtieth anniversary of service:

To DD with the consecrated voice
Serving the Saviour with a free-will choice,
Proclaiming the gospel in the words of song
Morning and evening the whole day long.

Singing to millions by the radio waves
Of the Christ she honors and the love that saves.
Still faithful her witness as the days go by
To the Saviour's mercy and a home on high.

We fellow workers of the said Del D
Appreciate and love her, as you can see.
She has shared in the victories, in the smiles and tears
In our radio broadcast for thirty years.

So we say, God bless her till the work is done
And the reapers gather with the setting sun.
May we all be singing on the glassy sea
With our Del Delker of the VOP!

I guess you can see why I consider that such a precious gift. I enjoyed working with The Chief, and I've enjoyed everyone else I've been privileged to serve with as well. Traveling together can be hectic, but I can honestly say that all of these people are still my friends. Many of them were able to attend the special concert the VOP produced in 2002 in honor of my fifty-fifth anniversary of service.

Jim Teel and I might still be working together if it hadn't been for the sudden and drastic changes that came about at the VOP in 1982. I'll be honest with you. I wasn't happy about what happened then. But even the events that seemed so bad at the time opened a wonderful new chapter of my life.

Chapter Twenty-Three

A transition of leadership happened at the VOP in 1969 when Dr. H. M. S. Richards—The Chief—retired from his role as director/speaker at age seventy-five. He was proud to be replaced by his son, H. M. S. Richards, Jr., whom we always referred to as Harold.

Harold had been part of the VOP team since 1961, and he and I had traveled together as "Group B" from 1961 to 1967, while The Chief and the King's Heralds were listed as "Group A." Harold, with a mischievous grin, always said that B stood for Best, but I know that he felt like he was trying to fill some very large shoes when he took over from his father. "Sometimes I feel like an ant stepping into the shoes of a dinosaur," he would say.

The Chief was beloved all over the world because of his courage in beginning a radio ministry, his powerful preaching, and his warm, personable way of meeting with people. It would have been hard for anyone to try to follow him, but there were things that made it especially hard for his namesake son. I remember one time when we arrived at a camp meeting and got out of the car. The administrator in charge of the meeting came out to greet us, and as soon as he saw Harold, his face fell. "Oh, I thought your dad was coming," was all he said. I felt like biting him in the leg!

Chapter Twenty-Three

We were driving along in the station wagon with the Braleys sometime later, when Harold looked at me and said, "They don't want to hear me. They want to hear my dad."

I let him have it. "Don't be silly," I said. "Forget your dad. You just need to be you. You have some wonderful qualities about you, and the people love you too."

I especially loved working in evangelism with Harold. When he would make an altar call at the end of his sermon, you could tell that he really loved the people and wanted them to accept salvation. And the people responded in droves. I don't know anyone I enjoyed doing altar calls with more than Harold.

He was also a great storyteller. But one of the things that set him apart from his dad even more was that he was a musician. Most people who are familiar with the Richards family remember the story of how Harold formed a jazz band while he was in high school, and how his father prayed for him late into the night. Well, when Harold felt the call to be a minister instead of a musician, he never lost his love of music. Many times he'd get together with a group of people and the first thing he'd say was, "Let's harmonize!" And we'd have an impromptu quartet or quintet or octet—depending on how many were there. One time at a camp meeting I came out onto the stage to sing, knowing that the next thing on the program was my music and then Harold's sermon, but when I looked at the speaker's chair, it was empty. I started to panic, wondering what had happened to him. Then I looked at the choir. There was Harold, singing his heart out in the baritone section!

Harold also took after his father in having a great sense of humor. When you travel with people on long trips, you get to know them pretty well, and one thing the Richardses soon learned about me is that I'm a bit absent-minded. I could easily misplace my head if it wasn't firmly attached to my neck! But the one thing I most often lost track of while traveling was my dark glasses. My traveling companions used to tease me unmercifully about it—and there was a time or two when I'm sure they purposely hid them just to tease me. But finally the day came when Harold got his comeuppance. It was in the middle '70s, when we were traveling with Calvin Taylor.

We headed out from our motel early one morning with a long drive ahead of us. Sixty miles down the road, Harold suddenly said, "Turn around! We've got to go back!"

"What's the matter," Calvin asked.

"Just turn around! I left my wallet under the mattress in the motel room."

And so a long day on the road suddenly got much longer. After that, whenever Harold would start to tease me about forgetting something all I had to say was, "Got your wallet, Harold?" and he'd have to leave me alone.

One of the funniest things I ever saw Harold do was at the Chesapeake camp meeting in Maryland. He was up preaching to a large crowd in an auditorium when a furious thunderstorm blew in. There was lightning, thunder, and pouring rain. It was raining so hard we thought the roof was about to cave in. All of a sudden the lights went out and it was pitch black. We all sat there in the darkness for about two minutes—it seemed like a lot longer of course—and then the lights came back on. As soon as the sound system came back on, Harold bent over to the mike and in his deep, booming voice said, "Wanna see me do it again?" That broke the tension and the crowd just roared with laughter. One of my happiest memories of traveling with Harold is when he brought his young teenage sons, Harold III (I called him "Three") and Jon. They were so much fun to go down slides with in the swimming pools. I just wish his daughter Mary could have been with us. She's a riot!

I don't know exactly how to tell you this next part, because it hurt me deeply when it happened, and I still have some strong feelings about it. The Chief always looked to his quartet, the King's Heralds, and me, and sometimes to other musicians as well, for musical support in his meetings. If there was an hour allotted, he'd always tell us to take half an hour. He felt music was an extremely important part of the ministry, because music can move people in ways that the spoken word cannot.

But by 1982, some of the people in leadership positions at the VOP didn't think that music was quite so important. And when some budgeting problems came up, they used that as a means to promote the idea of disbanding the department. There were other issues involved too. As in any organization, there had been some minor personality conflicts. But it came as a terrible shock when the vote was taken to dismiss all of the King's Heralds, plus my beloved accompanist, Jim Teel. I was called into the manager's office after the vote was taken and told that the quartet and Jim were leaving. "But we want to keep you," the manager said.

I just sat there in shock for a moment. What could this possibly mean? I had sung with prerecorded tracks a few times when an accompanist just couldn't be found, but it always made me uncomfortable. I need to have someone who can feel the music with me. So, when they told me Jim would no longer be able to travel with me, all I could think of to say was, "That's funny. The a cappella thing isn't in right now!"

With that, I just got up and walked out the door. I probably closed it a little harder than I should have, but I was really distraught. I heard later that when The Chief learned of the decision, he burst into tears.

Fortunately, I wasn't expected to sing a cappella from then on.

I have to say that I have loved working with every one of the many accompanists I've had the privilege of singing with through the years, and I'm still friends with every one of them who is still living. But one of the most special working relationships came about directly as a result of the changes at the VOP in 1982. It's a fascinating story that had begun to develop many years earlier.

One of the best-known composers in the show-business world is a man named Hugh Martin. Hugh was much in demand to write music for Broadway plays and Hollywood movies, especially in the 1930s and 1940s. All together he's composed more than 500 songs. His most famous tune ever is probably "Have Yourself a Merry Little Christmas," which he wrote for Judy Garland to sing in the movie *Meet Me in St. Louis* in 1941.

Hugh and Judy worked together on many productions, and he was often her accompanist for live performances. He has a way of playing the piano that's very smooth and that blended well with her voice. Hugh wasn't a religious person at all, but in 1960 as a result of some pain medication he was given, he suffered a complete nervous break-down and ended up in a hospital in England. While he was there, he found his way down to the little chapel and poured out his heart to God, asking for His help. Hugh told me the story of that life-changing day again a couple of years ago when I talked with him in preparation for a radio program. I'll let him tell it in his own words:

"I'll never forget it," he said. "It was probably the lowest moment of my life. I was so desperate. I couldn't sleep, I couldn't eat, and I couldn't stop crying. I cried for three weeks and finally roaming around the hospital, down in the basement, I found a sweet little chapel. It was nondenominational but it was very reverent and they had kneelers where we could kneel. I just skipped the kneeler and went right down on the floor on my face and I said Oh, my God, I don't know whether I'm going to live or die or go crazy, but if You are there, please come to me. I will serve You forever, if You will come and take me out of this miry pit."

After that prayer, things started to turn around for Hugh, and he was able to go back to work and finish the musical he was working on with Noel Coward.

Years later, after he had returned to the States, Hugh was listening to the radio one day and happened to hear a *Voice of Prophecy* program. I have to let him tell this part of the story, because he insists this is exactly how it was:

"I listened [to *The Voice of Prophecy*] for nine years, Del, and I listened because of you. This is not flattery, but I was not the least bit interested in sermons or messages or the Bible, I still was not there yet. But your voice captivated me, and I remember thinking, If only I could be her accompanist.

"Del it was your voice that captivated me. I was not ready for sermons and Bible readings and all those really important things. Not that you weren't important too. But you were very important because otherwise I don't think I would have been pulled into the whole atmosphere of heaven. But your voice entranced me. Since Judy Garland I'd never heard anyone I really wanted to play for and be the accompanist for, but when I heard you sing, I thought, *Oh, if only I could be her accompanist I'd be happy forever.*"

Chapter Twenty-Three

I hope you understand that I'm not telling you about this as any sort of bragging or taking credit to myself. I'm just pleased that the Lord was able to use my voice to speak to a soul who was searching.

Hugh continued listening to the radio, but never contacted me until after another dramatic moment in his life. This one happened in a hospital too. He had to go in for a checkup, and he had reserved a private room, but somehow when he arrived at the hospital he heard an inner voice say to him, "Share your room." It wasn't an audible voice, but still the message came through loud and clear. At first he argued—Lord, You know I went to a lot of trouble to reserve this private room. But it still came through loud and clear: "Hugh, share your room."

The man he ended up sharing his room with turned out to be a Seventh-day Adventist minister named William Lester! Hugh was so impressed with that man's devotion to the Lord that they soon were involved in Bible study, and in 1979, Hugh was baptized. It wasn't long after that that we met, and he told me of his longstanding desire to be able to accompany me.

Well, of course, at that time Jim Teel was traveling with me, it wasn't often that I needed Hugh. Nevertheless, in 1980, Hugh moved up to Newbury Park, to be near the VOP office, just in case he might be needed. He lived there for two years, and we'd visit from time to time, but he finally figured out that he wasn't going to be needed as my accompanist enough to warrant his staying in the area.

Then, in 1982, when I realized that changes might be coming in the music department, I felt impressed one day to go by and talk to Hugh. He was just going out the door of his apartment when I arrived, and I asked where he was going. "I'm going down to the office to tell them that I'll be moving out. I guess there's no purpose in my staying here any longer, since you don't need me to accompany you very often."

I didn't know at the time just how things were going to turn out at the VOP, but I had a feeling that changes were coming, so I said to Hugh, "Just wait a month or two longer. I have a feeling there's some changes coming. You've been here for two years, just give it a couple more months."

He agreed, and it wasn't long after that that I ended up needing an accompanist.

Because Hugh was well up in years, and a bit frail, he couldn't go on extended itineraries with me, but over the next four summers we did a series of tours together, going from state to state by airplane, playing and singing, and letting Hugh give his testimony of how the Lord had led in his life. People at the meetings loved him instantly, and he returned their affection. We had some truly wonderful times together, traveling for the Lord and sharing the gospel. Hugh remains a close friend, and was able to come to the taping of my fifty-fifth anniversary video in June 2002, where he accompanied me as I sang the Christian version of his famous song. It's called "Have Yourself a Blessed Little Christmas," and it's now included with every copy of the original "Have Yourself a Merry Little Christmas" that's sold as sheet music.

During those years I also traveled some with Janice Wright, another talented accompanist. She was a delightful traveling companion who always managed to find the best ice cream parlor in any city we visited—along with a lot of other interesting places to see.

Meanwhile, Harold had begun to take Phil and Joey Draper with him as musicians when he did evangelism. In 1986, Phil became my accompanist, and we've had some really great times working together. Especially our trip to Australia and New Zealand.

Chapter Twenty-Four

In 1985, Phil Draper joined the staff as Development Director. His wife Joey happens to have a beautiful, rich contralto voice that people love to listen to. I think some people were watching us to see if the green-eyed monster would rear its ugly head, but believe me—it never did. Joey and I have always been supportive of each other's talent. There is no room in God's work for jealousy. As far as both of us were, and are, concerned the more people to sing God's praises, the better. Phil, Joey, and I are the best of friends, and always will be. They are fun and caring people. Since there were so many places to cover, I and an accompanist were sent out by ourselves, and Harold Richards took Phil and Joey with him, providing music almost everywhere he preached.

In 1986, Phil became my accompanist. Our first trip was to Australia and New Zealand. We had a great time in those countries and fell in love with the people and the gorgeous scenery. Phil has an amazing gift at the keyboard. He can listen to a song once and sit right down and play it, in most any key. Some people even suggested that I ought to retire and let Phil and Joey travel together representing the VOP.

I suppose the time for me to "hang it up" is soon. I've always said that I want to keep singing for the Lord as long as He gives me strength, but I hope I'll have the good sense to quit when the right time comes. Somewhere I picked up this definition of old age: "Old age occurs the moment you realize there isn't something very wonderful about to happen just around the corner. In some people this occurs very soon, in others not at all." Frankly, I still think there's something wonderful coming just around the corner—every day.

Speaking of old age, people are always curious about my age. When I tell them I've been singing for The Voice of Prophecy for fifty-five years, I can see them start to do the math in their heads, and then I smile and say, "Of course I was only four years old when I started!"

I suppose you'll be able to figure out my true age by some of the clues you'll find in this book, but that won't be because I out-and-out told you how old I was. My mother taught me that if a woman will tell you her age, she'll tell you anything. And believe me, I've got a few secrets I'm not telling anyone. Ken Wade tells me that when people hear that he's helping me write this book, they often ask him, "Well, how old is Del, anyhow?"

I guess they figure they can sneak right past me and get the information from my biographer. But Ken just looks them in the eye and says, "I could tell you. But then I'd have to kill you!" Fortunately, he hasn't had to kill anyone yet. I don't know how old most people think I am, but I do remember the little old man who came up to greet me in Australia. He looked to be about ninety-five, and in a loud voice he announced, "Del Delker, I've always wanted to meet you. Why, I can remember hearing you sing on the radio when I was just a wee little boy!"

Don't think Phil Draper hasn't had some fun with that story through the years! And he also likes to tease me about the time, just recently, when I was at a meeting with J. L. Tucker's grandson William Tucker. We were reminiscing about the old days at The Quiet Hour, and Bill asked me how old he was when I met him there. I told him he was about two years old.

Well, one of the young boys in the congregation that day must have looked at Bill and thought he was pretty old, because he tugged on his daddy's arm and pointed to me and asked, "Daddy, is that

Sister White?"—referring to Ellen G. White, who died at a ripe old age about a decade before I was born! Oh well, I take some consolation in the comment of another young boy who came up to me after a meeting recently. "Your voice sounds younger than you are!" he said.

As I said, Phil became my accompanist in 1986, and I admit I gave him a run for his money. Remember that when Wayne Hooper and I would audition potential accompanists, we'd set a difficult piece of music in front of them and see how well they could play it the first time through. Well, Phil has a wonderful ear for music, but he doesn't sight read a whole lot better than I do—which is not at all. So I was a bit leery. How could I develop a repertoire with him?

What I didn't know was that Phil already had a solution for that problem. I think he and Joey had one of the most complete collections of my record albums owned by anyone. And they'd listened to them over and over. And Joey had sung most of the songs in evangelistic meetings—with Phil at the keyboard. He already knew most of the songs I wanted to sing, and could play them in whatever key I chose.

So Phil accompanied Harold and me on our six-week trip to visit camp meetings in New Zealand and Australia in 1986, and he and I hit it off marvelously right from the start. His sense of humor and mine are very similar, and soon we were trading one-liners and keeping each other in stitches. Once Phil gets started, he can keep popping up with smart remarks one after another until he has everybody laughing. In fact, in a small group he steals the show from me quite often, and I'll get a pouty look on my face and tell the others, "Don't laugh at him! It just encourages him."

But seriously, I've learned to really appreciate Phil, because he not only accompanies me while I sing, but he's there for me when I need him for other things as well. In recent years, when I was having so much trouble with my hip popping out of joint, people always knew to call on Phil if he was anywhere nearby, because he seemed to know how to help me get it back in place. He's often been the one to take me to and from the hospital, and he and Joey are both quick to make themselves available whenever I need help.

On our 1986 trip we went to Auckland, New Zealand, first. We flew out of Los Angeles two days before Christmas, but didn't land in New Zealand until late afternoon on the 25th, because of crossing the International Date Line on our thirteen-hour flight. We literally had to hit the ground running. I was singing at a convocation just two hours after we landed! We stayed at the North New Zealand camp meeting for six days. During that time Harold Richards preached seventeen sermons, and Phil and I performed an average of fifteen songs a day. Talk about a baptism by fire! It's a good thing we already had a repertoire of over 100 songs to choose from.

After that camp meeting we had several days free before our first appointment in Australia. Harold wanted to use the time to travel around visiting amateur radio operators that he had talked to from the U. S. Harold was an avid "ham" who loved to use short-wave radio to talk to people all over the world. Wherever he went, he could count on meeting someone he'd spoken to. Phil and I were much more interested in seeing the country than visiting people only Harold knew, so we planned to use our free time as vacation time. We traveled by boat, plane, helicopter, ships, train, and a rented car, and had a wonderful time touring both of New Zealand's islands. I found out that if you really want to see a place, Phil's the guy to go with. He's always coming up with ideas—some of them great but others, well let's just say you have to sort the good from the best. The idea that got me in trouble, though, was one I came up with myself.

There are more sheep than people in New Zealand, and one day I decided I wanted to pet a sheep. We stopped beside a large pasture surrounded by a rail fence, and Phil helped me climb over. Even with his help though, I somehow cracked a rib getting across. The pain would be a bother for all the rest of the trip, but it didn't stop me from enjoying what we did. A saying that's stuck with me through the years is, "Joy is not the absence of pain, but the presence of God."

We certainly felt the Lord's presence as we went from place to place. The Holy Spirit ministered powerfully through Harold's preaching and through our music. I remember one man who came up to Harold after the meeting and told how he had been a Christian for only a few years. Then he said, "But I felt I was just going through the motions. Until today, that is. Your sermon, Pastor Richards, touched my heart. I've given my life anew to Christ. I feel like I'm back on the cutting edge again!"

In Australia we traveled down the beautiful coast to Brisbane, Melbourne, and Sydney, then crossed over to Tasmania. There, at the close of a morning meeting, I sang Wayne Hooper's wonderful song, "The Lord Is Coming, Are You Ready?" Afterward a couple came up to talk to me. The husband confessed that he hadn't even wanted to be there, but went along just to please his wife. That song touched a chord in his heart, and he rededicated himself to serving the Lord.

It's experiences like these that make all the miles, jet lag, and lost luggage that inevitably come with travel worthwhile. Most of all, we're looking forward to the trip to heaven, where we'll get to meet these friends from far countries again.

Chapter Twenty-Five

How I pled with Phil not to leave The Voice of Prophecy in the fall of 1988! After Australia, we'd had many more wonderful trips together, across the U. S. and to Bermuda, accompanying Harold Richards to camp meetings, Harvest Time Rallies, evangelistic meetings, and college spiritual-emphasis weeks.

I guess all that travel was part of the problem. Because Phil's a family man, and their little daughter Brittany, whom they had adopted in 1980, was getting to an age when he knew it was especially important to be there for her. So, when he received a call to another Christian ministry, with the promise that he wouldn't have to be away from home so much, he took it.

Cry and plead as I might, I just couldn't persuade Phil to stay on as my accompanist. Fortunately La Voz de la Esperanza, the Spanish version of our ministry, had recently hired a new organist named Fernando (Ferdie) Westre, an excellent young musician. He was very quick to learn, so we hurriedly put together a repertoire and went on the road south of the equator, just as I'd done when Phil first traveled with me. We began our forty-two-hour flight (including a six-hour layover in England) on November 14. This time we were going to South Africa.

My good friends Gordon and Phyllis Henderson, whom I'd traveled with in 1967 after Wedgwood, joined us for this African trip,

along with Harold Richards. The Hendersons had been devoting
their time to evangelistic meetings for several years as part of the
VOP team, and I'd worked with them often.

Phyllis was such a delight to travel with. She had a wonderful
disposition, and she was also a great organizer. A few years later,
when Phyllis passed to her rest, I wrote this tribute to her:

My Friend, Phyllis

What do I think of when I think of Phyllis Henderson
(besides her great big smile that spread all over her face?).
Dedication—that's what! She was willing to be used of God.
And how God used her at home and in her travels all over the
world! Part of her ministry was in the limelight as a singer in
duets with her husband Gordon, and as a pianist and organist.

Phyllis did not have a "star" complex. She often considered others more talented, and she rejoiced when they praised
the Lord with their gifts. But I know very few persons who
can do as many different things as she could do.

In evangelistic campaigns she kept everyone organized,
acting as secretary of the campaign. At the same time, she
was a superb visitor in the homes of interested people who
came to our meetings. I visited in many homes with her in
countless campaigns through the years. I remember a few
times when people were not very receptive to a visit at first,
but I saw them melt into a puddle of butter after she flashed
one of her toothy smiles at them. They couldn't resist her
love and friendship. People saw the love of Jesus in her.

Phyllis's health wasn't great for a number of years, but she
would go on trips anyway, motivated by her love to be where
the action for Christ was. I've seen her travel when anyone
else would have checked into a hospital! Sheer grit and deter-
mination! Phil Draper, one of the musicians who went with us
on a number of trips, once said, "Phyllis would go on a trip if
she had to strap an iron lung to the wing of a plane."

But no matter how she felt, that sweet smile would be
there. I used to think as I watched her sing or play that she

looked like a blonde angel. Believe me, she meant what she was singing or playing, and she loved every minute of witnessing for Christ.

Phyllis was my good friend. She was one of the few people I could share things with and feel safe. Although we both knew how to be dignified when we needed to, we also enjoyed giggling together and seeing the funny side of life.

Sometimes we argued and even disagreed with each other. She had a strong mind (and I've been accused of the same!), so sometimes we had to straighten each other out! I tried to get her to slow down and not overextend herself, but my arguments usually fell on deaf ears!

Phyllis was a loving wife, mother, daughter, sister, friend, and servant of God. She was a good secretary, cook (nobody made spaghetti sauce like Phyllis), homemaker, financier, seamstress, and musician. She loved the Lord and served Him well for many years, but she died before she was 60. Much too soon! She packed a lot into her short life. And someday soon, when our Lord returns and says, "Wake up, Phyllis, it's time to go home," Phyllis will pop out of her resting place, flash one of her toothy smiles, and say, "OK, Lord! I'm ready. Let's go!"

Our trip to South Africa was like most of our itineraries: a whirlwind of activity that included almost getting blown away by a real whirlwind! OK, true confession is good for the soul, they say. So here goes: Sometimes I wear a wig.

Not often, mind you. But there are times when you arrive at a place just minutes before you're to go on stage, and there's just no time for fiddling with one's tresses. That's when it's a good thing to have a hairdo in a box!

Is the Lord concerned with such little details in our lives? Remember the preacher who turned my aunts away from the church by worrying himself over women who were so sinful as to have permanents (or "premadies" as he called them)? I wonder what he would think of an Adventist singer wearing a wig occasionally!

Chapter Twenty-Five

Well, I think I have a little clue as to whether the Lord is concerned with such things or not because of something that happened to me in Cape Town. I was seriously considering wearing a wig to the Sabbath afternoon program. I was just too weary to do my own hair. But then I heard one of those little internal voices that you only hear occasionally, and it seemed to be telling me not to put the wig on this time. And before the day was over, I was very glad I listened to that voice. The wig probably would have ended up somewhere in Antarctica if I'd worn it.

When we arrived at the meeting, 6,000 people had gathered in the grandstand, and they were somewhat sheltered from the wind. But the platform where the speakers and singers were was out in the open and took the full force of near-hurricane winds. Poor Phyllis, as thin and light as she was, nearly got blown right off the stage. If it had not been for the quick thinking of Ferdie, who jumped up and grabbed on to her, she would have taken quite a fall.

The fact that I was spared the embarrassment of having a wig blow off seems small by comparison, but maybe there's a lesson in it—about God's care for us in big things and small.

We had reserved the last two days of our trip for sightseeing, but by that time Gordon was too exhausted and just wanted to rest. Harold, as usual, wanted to use the time to visit with radio friends. So Phyllis, Ferdie, and I flew up to Kruger National Park to spend two days viewing the wildlife. It was an interesting experience, as the animals roamed freely; it was we people who were in cages, because we couldn't even open the door of our car. Poor Phyllis was trying so hard to get a picture of a lion. She leaned out with her camera but bumped something, and the batteries fell out on the ground. That ended her picture taking. She couldn't even open the door far enough to retrieve the batteries.

The next year, 1989, was another busy travel year, taking me to destinations in the U. S. and Canada. Near the end of the year I joined the Hendersons again for a two-week evangelistic series in Chattanooga, Tennessee. By that time I had completed forty-two years of service at the VOP, and it was time to start thinking about slowing down a bit—maybe even retiring.

Chapter Twenty-Six

Bob Edwards and I both went to work at the VOP in 1947, and both of us retired on January 1, 1990.

Retired. Ha!

It's not like I all of a sudden hung up my traveling shoes and sat down by the swimming pool to soak up the sun. I still haven't quit traveling and singing—at people's request. You see, that's what I tell people—now when they ask me to go anywhere, they have to say "please," not just give me orders.

Not that I'm complaining about having been told where to go for so many years. Almost all of my experience in serving my Lord through the ministry of the VOP has been positive. But I wouldn't be telling the whole story if I didn't confess that there were some rough spots along the way.

The fact that the others in the music department didn't think they needed me when I first arrived was one of those spots. Then there were times when it seemed like the administration played favorites. All of us musicians worked hard—holding down regular jobs at the office during the week, then traveling most weekends and taking extended trips every summer. It didn't leave us much spare time. Eventually a policy was instituted that let the quartet members take an extra week of paid vacation every year to partially make up for the missed weekends and holidays with their families.

It was probably just an oversight when the action was taken, but nobody bothered to mention that I traveled just as much and put in just as long hours as the others. So I wasn't included in the policy.

The next time I was ready to take a vacation, I went to see the manager. "Are you going to let me have an extra week of vacation like the quartet?" I asked.

The question caught him by surprise. "Well, uh, I guess that wasn't voted in the policy," he hedged.

"That's OK," I said. "I'll just make it my policy. I'm taking the extra week, and you're going to make sure I get paid for it." With that I turned on my heel and left.

And I got paid.

I guess it sometimes pays to have a little hardheaded German blood running through your veins. After all, fair is fair.

But really, money wasn't ever a big issue with me. From the day I left Greyhound to devote my life to serving the Lord, I've never been in it for the money. Honestly. One of our top church administrators, Pastor Robert H. Pierson, discovered that one day in the '70s when he sat with a committee that was reviewing salaries. When my name came up, he looked at the figures and his eyes bugged out. "What's this?" he asked our manager. "This woman travels all over the world representing The Voice of Prophecy, and you aren't even paying her top secretarial wage? That's wrong!"

The manager didn't know how to respond. But my wages did go up after that. The Chief came by my office and told me what had happened and with tears in his eyes apologized to me that no one had stood up for me earlier. I wasn't aware of it—I was eating three meals a day, so I hadn't seen any reason to complain about my wages.

In 1993 Harold Richards asked me whether I would like to go back to Brazil one more time. There was no way I could turn him down. It would be my fifth trip to that great country, and I wanted to see my friends down there again.

I said Yes. But with a caveat. "I'm retired now," I reminded him. "I want to see the schedule first and make sure there'll be enough time for me to catch my breath between songs!"

What a thrill it was to meet Pastor Roberto Rabello again and to watch the reactions of the huge crowds when he would stand to speak. At age eighty-four, the years of hard work and exhausting travel schedules had taken their toll. But he was still able to meet us in most of the cities we visited. Everywhere he was honored as the founder of the Brazilian *Voice of Prophecy* broadcast half a century earlier.

Since I've always been interested in and loved young people, it thrilled me to see how active the Brazilian youth are in church events. Many of our meetings were held in large stadiums, and the Pathfinder youth group provided ushers to help with crowd control. In the city of Salvador, a thousand Pathfinders marched in the huge Fonte Nova Stadium. And whenever there was a baptism (and believe me, there were many—about 20,000 were baptized in meetings all across the country), the young people were there to help the candidates in and out of the baptismal tank.

On this trip I traveled with Lonnie and Jeannie Melashenko, and what a wonderful time we had together. Phil Draper also joined us, taking time off from his other job to travel with me and accompany me when I sang. (In 1995 he returned to the VOP as development director and has been my accompanist ever since.) The Brazilian King's Heralds were also part of our group.

Lonnie had just recently been appointed to be the new director-speaker of the VOP, working together with Harold Richards. I first met Lonnie when he was a little two-year-old towhead. His father, Joe, was singing bass with the King's Heralds when I first arrived at the VOP. Lonnie brings a rich musical heritage with him. The Melashenko Family Singers—which includes him, his parents, his four brothers, and their wives, plus many nieces and nephews, are a popular attraction at many gatherings these days.

Little did I realize that Lonnie, the adorable little towhead I met in 1947, would grow up to be the director-speaker of our ministry, and that he would consent to sing duets with a pioneer songbird like me! People have told us we blend well together.

Harold Richards was joined in Brazil by Gordon Henderson and a reunited King's Heralds group—the quartet as it had been in 1962 had been giving concerts for the past couple of years as a thirtieth-anniversary celebration. After an initial meeting in the city of Salvador, Harold's group went north into the steamy jungles, while our group headed for the cooler southern cities of Belo Horizonte, Vitória, Curitiba, and Pôrto Alegre. We then reunited for a final weekend in Rio. Unfortunately, while he was on this trip, Harold got typhoid fever, which seemed to get quite a bit worse after his return to the United States. He never fully regained his strength after that setback.

Our very last meeting in Brazil was in an outdoor sports stadium in what I feel is the most beautiful city in the world, Rio de Janeiro. As I was singing on the huge platform looking up at the starry sky, I could see the "Christ the Redeemer" statue with arms outstretched and all lit up atop Corcovado mountain. This statue dominates the city and always gives me goose bumps.

I realized that this would probably be my last trip to Brazil. To conclude our program, the Arautos do Rei (Brazilian King's Heralds) sang, "Lift up the trumpet, and loud let it ring: Jesus is coming again!" And I, along with tens of thousands of others, responded, "Even so come, Lord Jesus!"

Since 1993 I've tried to limit my travels to shorter trips that don't involve so many stops, and that has enabled me to continue my ministry. At Phil Draper's urging, I joined him and the Melashenkos in the Cayman Islands in early 2002. That's when I discovered that my name is known in Hell. That's no joke, actually. There's a place on Grand Cayman Island named Hell, and when I was there, one of the saleswomen came up to me and asked, "Aren't you Del Delker?" I assured her that I was, and she told me how much she had enjoyed my music through the years. I'm not sure how glad I should be to be recognized in a place called Hell, but I am glad my music has had a ministry there! And I wasn't the only one recognized there. Lonnie and Jeannie can also brag that they were recognized in Hell!

Another time when I was recognized—years earlier—was also a bit questionable. Should I be happy or not? I've never decided for sure. Here's what happened: I was getting ready to go to the stage and sing at a large meeting and stopped by the ladies' room to freshen up. The place was empty except for a chubby cleaning woman. She looked at me and said, "Is you Del Delker? You sure do looks like Del Delker. Is you Del Delker? No, you's not Del Delker. You sure do look like her, but she's not very pretty. You's a lot prettier than her. She's not very pretty, but she's sweet lookin'."

I never did have the heart to tell her who I was. And I've never figured out whether to take her comment as a compliment or not.

Of course there have been many other humorous events in my many years of travel. One of my favorites happened at a camp meeting not long ago, when I was asked to tell a children's story. I called all the children down front. This was at a huge meeting, and hundreds of kids came forward. Just as I got ready to start the story, one little boy stood up and waved his hand back and forth, "Miss Delker, Miss Delker," he said.

"Yes, what can I do for you?" I asked.

"I have to go to the bathroom," he said. "Please can you wait—don't do anything until I get back!" And with that, he took off running.

Some of the adults in the congregation heard what was going on and started laughing. I just looked out over the sea of faces and said, "When you gotta go, you gotta go." That brought the house down. I think some people were still laughing when the little boy came back and I was able to tell my story.

Being single and not having a close family to call your own is not an easy way to go through life. Don't think I've never wished I had followed my dream of marrying a young ministerial student and settling down to a fairly normal life as a pastor's wife. But that doesn't seem to be what God called me to.

I still have a lot of joy thinking of the years I spent helping Bernice raise her three girls. And I stay in touch with each of her daughters pretty regularly, so it's not like I never had any family at all. (Unfortunately, after a series of strokes that began in 1971, Bernice's health has deteriorated to the point where she hardly recognizes anyone who comes to visit her anymore. She's in a nursing home in Washington, near Beth, who sees to it she's well taken care of.)

Chapter Twenty-Six

I've always considered ministry to children on and off the plat-form one of the most important things anyone can do. A forty-year-old woman recently came up to me and told me that I had picked her up and held her when she was five years old, and that she had always remembered that—when things had gone bad in her life, she had hearkened back to that day and taken new courage to go on, feeling that she was someone special to the Lord just because of the little attention I had shown her so many years ago.

The amazing thing to me is that my music has often been used of the Lord to touch young lives. One of my good friends through the years has been Deanna Davis. I first met her when she was a teenager, and she's now in her fifties. She's given her life in service to the Lord as a writer and editor, but it could have been very different. Here's how she explained it a few years ago:

"My parents were divorced before I was born. My father was an alcoholic and a convicted felon. He had served time for crimes including child molestation. At age thirteen, I became one of his victims. My mother had been physically and verbally abused as a child. She had not had an opportu-nity to learn any other way of parenting. I received nearly daily beatings. My only sibling, an older sister, died the night before my eleventh birthday. My aunts cleaned out her room and moved my stuff in. They left a couple of her things they thought I could use—a radio and a record player. I began to listen to the VOP and collect Del Delker's albums, which I played by the hour. She became my surrogate mother. And H. M. S. Richards, the grandfather I never knew.

"When I was fourteen and feeling very depressed and hopeless, I heard Del sing 'The Love of God' at the Oregon camp meeting, and as she sang I wondered if that love 'that goes beyond the highest star and reaches to the lowest hell' could reach me too. I'm not just sure how it happened, but suddenly I knew that God loved me and that He made me for a purpose. My life was not a mistake. By the time I turned my attention back to Del, she was singing,

'Could we with ink the ocean fill,
And were the skies of parchment made,
Were every stalk on earth a quill,
And every man a scribe by trade,
To write the love of God above,
Would drain the ocean dry.
Nor could the scroll contain the whole,
Though stretched from sky to sky.'

"I'd never heard a gospel song about writing before. I knew I could never sing like Del, but I could write. Maybe I could spend my life writing about the love of God the way Del has spent hers singing about it. Not long after that eventful day, I wrote to Del. I bought a special tablet of paper that had blue and pink and yellow and white pages. It was a long letter, and I went through the colors a number of times. And then I mailed it. Some weeks later, I received her answer. I still have it."

Deanna told me that when she shared her story with a psychologist, he said, "I believe Del saved your life."

I'm just glad I was able to be there for her.

Another young person who was touched by my music has become my good friend. Moses Brown was born in Florida, the product of the rape of a little fifteen-year-old girl. He was taken into a foster home and later adopted by his foster parents. These folks listened to the VOP and played my records in the home, but Moses says that he didn't care to listen to me at first. He would much rather have been listening to Diana Ross. But somehow over the years the words and music began to speak to him, and finally he gave his heart to the Lord. Now he is employed in a public high school. They send unruly, defiant young people to him for counsel, discipline, and guidance. On weekends he leads out in a very special ministry called Feed Our Children (F. O. C.) that supplies food to unwanted and disadvantaged children. Moses has a nice singing voice, and his wife, Jeanette, is an accomplished musician. Together they use their musical talents to help raise funds for the F. O. C. ministry. It's just amazing how when you share what you know of God's love, it touches lives and then touches others through those lives!

Stephanie Dawn also exemplifies this. I first met this blind-from-birth girl when she was only four years old. She tells me that one of her earliest memories is of walking around with a tape player, listening to my music. She's become a Christian musician of considerable reknown now, having been invited to sing at the Kennedy Center in Washington, D.C., twice already. I'm sure she feels superior to me because I've never been invited to sing at the Kennedy Center. Why, I'll never know! We've become fast friends through the years, and there have been many times when I've had the chance to encourage her and give her guidance, and she never fails to cheer me up and try to give me guidance. I love her sense of humor, and we giggle a lot and tease each other. We are often in contact by phone. Stephanie is now the ripe old age of twenty-two, and I admire her devotion and her desire that all the talent the Lord has given her be used to His glory.

All of us have some ability that we can devote to serving the Lord and helping others. I've always admired the attitude of Milton Alfonso, who lives in Brazil. He owns a very prosperous insurance company, and he has donated millions of dollars through the years to help spread the gospel in his country. I believe he has even been the one financing several Voice of Prophecy projects there, including sponsoring travel when I have been invited to sing there.

One day one of Milton's friends asked him why he is so generous in supporting God's work. "Don't you think you're overdoing it?" he asked. "Why do you do it?"

Milton's response was simple, but poignant, and I've always remembered it. He simply said, "I'm in a hurry."

What he meant, of course, is that he's in a hurry for God's work to be finished so we all can go home.

I'm in a hurry too. How about you?

Chapter Twenty-Seven

There are so many more things I could tell you about my life. And so many I've forgotten. (I tell people I have a photographic memory, but I keep running out of film! I also tell them I'm now in the snapdragon part of life—part of me has lost its snap, and the other part is draggin'!) But seriously, I could no doubt fill another book this length with stories of God's love and leading. As I look back over my fifty-five years of serving God, I can only marvel at how He can take a life and make it over—better.

God often uses simple things to change lives. A word, a smile, a song, a Bible text—some little evidence of God's care that takes a person and points them in a different direction. Knowing this has encouraged me through the years to do everything I can to be a positive influence on those around me. You never know when opportunity will knock. It happened to Phil Draper and me in the back seat of a taxi cab in New York once. As we rode along, I could tell that the driver was a kind, caring man, but that life was starting to get him down. Somehow I felt impressed to talk to him. "Are you a Christian?" I asked.

"Well, I believe in God," he responded. "And I'm quite interested in spiritual things."

That was all the opening I needed. As we continued talking, I began to hope that we'd have a good, long ride with him so I could get him signed up for a Bible correspondence course. I leaned over to Phil and whispered, "Pray that we'll have to stop at every stop light!" Phil prayed. And we stopped at every light. This gave me the time to get Edwin's name and address so we could enroll him in the Bible Correspondence School.

I didn't think much more about it for a time, because I often sign people up for the Bible course while I'm traveling. But then a few weeks later a letter came to the Bible school from Edwin. "Hi, you all, I have to tell you that I love you all very much. Miss Del Delker was in my cab with a gentleman one day and enrolled me in the New Life Guides. In all my life, I never had understood the Bible. But Jesus was telling me to listen for a long time. The New Life Guides are very good. Many things I did not know, now I know. I was so surprised."

He went on to say that he was no longer driving a cab, but was looking for work and wherever he went he was trying to help people. Later he wrote to me to tell me he'd gotten a job as a doorman, and that he used his constant contact with people as a way to share God's love. The girls in the Bible School told me that he was almost ready for baptism.

So often you don't see immediate results like that when you share with someone, but occasionally you do. So I keep speaking a good word for the Lord, both on stage and off. I still correspond with a young German girl named Uta that Phil and I met while riding in a van on the way home from the airport a year or so ago. She had been here in the U. S. as an exchange student, and since she returned home we've continued to develop our friendship by correspondence. I've been able to share my faith in Jesus with her several times. I gave Uta all twenty-six lessons of the Discover Bible Course to take back to Germany with her. I pray that she will read them. So I always encourage people to strike up a conversation—especially if you sense the Holy Spirit is telling you you're with someone who might be open to spiritual things.

As I look back over my life, I trace my own joy and all the blessings that have come my way to one young man—a U. S. Marine—who spoke up and invited me to a place I didn't want to go. I wonder what my life would have been like if Bob Thompson hadn't had the courage, and the perseverance, to keep urging me to go to The Quiet Hour that night.

I never dreamed before that that God could take my life and use it to bless others. But He did. And He continues to do so. He can do the same for you. Whoever you are. Wherever you are. I have often enjoyed watching the fireworks on the Fourth of July. But oh, my friends, the spectacular scene we are soon going to witness when Christ returns will be a sight we can't even imagine. And then to live with Him for all eternity! Here is a description of eternal life that has been a favorite of mine for many years:

> All the treasures of the universe will be open to the study of God's redeemed. Unfettered by mortality, they wing their tireless flight to worlds afar—worlds that thrilled with sorrow at the spectacle of human woe and rang with songs of gladness at the tidings of a ransomed soul. With unutterable delight the children of earth enter into the joy and the wisdom of unfallen beings. . . .
>
> And the years of eternity, as they roll, will bring richer and still more glorious revelations of God and of Christ. As knowledge is progressive, so will love, reverence, and happiness increase.

I hope you'll be there to share that wonderful experience with Jesus and all the redeemed.

Please pray this prayer with me: Precious Jesus, the heartbeat of Your coming is so real, and I claim You as my Savior and my Master for all eternity. And I claim Your precious promise, "Surely I come quickly."

Even so, come, Lord Jesus!